FUTURES TRADING

THE ULTIMATE BEGINNERS GUIDE TO MAKE MONEY ONLINE INVESTING IN THE FUTURES MARKET. MASTER THE PSYCHOLOGY, RISK AND MONEY MANAGEMENT AND LEARN EFFECTIVE DAY TRADING STRATEGIES

MARK SWING

CONTENTS

INTRODUCTION

Brief History of Futures

Chicago turned into the center of commercial exchange during the 1840s as it was connected by a network of railroads and telegraph lines. The Chicago Board of Trade was established in 1848 that gave rise to the futures contract. The foremost futures contracts were developed for commodities, agricultural commodities in particular.

The popular story about futures is that they were developed to assist farmers' hedge against variations in price of their cultivated crops. Futures can serve as a valuable instrument for hedging market-specific risk and can also be utilized for the usual trading and speculation. Traders can attain massive profits from futures, which are a leveraged product. However, they are also quite risky.

Corn was the foremost futures contract to be traded, followed by soybeans, wheat, cocoa, cotton, pork cattle, orange juice, sugar, and several other items. Gradually, contracts for other products were formulated. Futures trading started entering other markets by the 1970s.

Futures Contract

A futures contract is basically a legal agreement regarding purchasing or selling a particular instrument at a specified price and at a given time in the future. The core asset of a futures contract may be commodities, stocks, bonds, currencies and other instruments. There are standardized conditions of a futures contract in terms of quantity and date of delivery. Trading between buyers and sellers is supported by the exchanges. Cash is to be presented by traders if they wish to carry out futures trading, and this is typically known as margin in futures trading. It is important to maintain an appropriate margin for the continuation of the trade.

Margin

To carry out futures trading, it is important for traders to have adequate margin. This is dependent on the type of future being traded and the number of contracts. Three kinds of margin need to be comprehended if one wants to understand margin in its entirety. These are:

- Initial Margin
- Clearing Margin
- Maintenance Margin.

Initial Margin

Initial margin refers to the amount needed to carry out a futures trade. It is usually the exchanges themselves that determine this amount. The actual exposure of the trade may be higher than the initial margin. In case the loss of a trade becomes more than the initial margin, the broker may give a margin call. When a margin call is made by a broker, it is expected that traders will post margin to bring up the account for that day. Most of the futures accounts are marked to market by brokers on a daily basis. This suggests that futures contracts are examined again at the close of each trading day. The profit and loss are added and deducted from the margin every day.

Example of Initial Margin

The exchanges determine the initial margin for futures, and typically, the amount constitutes around 5% to 15% of the contract. This amount may be different for each broker. Consider the following as an example.

A trader is seeking to establish a wheat contract for $50,000, and the initial margin for futures contracts of wheat is fixed at 10%. The trader will have to post the initial margin amount of merely $5,000. A vital point regarding the initial margin is that it may be modified by the exchanges if there is an increase in volatility.

Clearing Margin

Clearing margin refers to the money that brokerages and institutional firms should have to fulfill futures contracts with their clients. It is basically a kind of capital security awarded to brokers so as to make sure that client trades are carried out.

Maintenance Margin

The maintenance margin refers to the least amount of cash that should be maintained in a trader's account to ensure that trade remains open for a futures contract. When the net value of the account becomes less than the maintenance margin, then the broker will make a margin call. After a margin call is made, more funds should be added by the trader so that the account value exceeds the minimum threshold.

Settlement in Futures

When a futures position is entered by a trader, he/she can

choose from 4 different alternatives regarding how to settle the trade.

- Straight Cash Settlement
- Physical Delivery
- Expiration
- Regular Closeout

Straight Cash Settlement

At the expiry of the futures contract, cash for the transaction is paid or received by those who are party to the transaction. This happens most often when physical delivery is not possible for a particular future.

Physical Delivery

Physical delivery is quite rare in the present times. Actual physical delivery of the underlying asset is made for not even 1% of futures contract. When it does happen, the seller delivers the amount given in the contract to the actual exchange. This can occur with commodities, but is quite rare.

For example, consider a situation in which you had 1 contract on wheat futures. Wheat futures have a typical contract size of 5000 bushels. At the contract's expiry, physical delivery of 5000 bushels of wheat can be taken.

Though only cash settlements will be made by majority of the brokers, it should be noted that a small proportion of brokers does take physical delivery. Most people give preference to over wheat at any time.

Expiration

The expiration date of a futures contract signifies the point when the trading of the futures ends and the ultimate settlement price for that particular period is obtained. Usually, a trader's position is expired by majority of the brokers by ending their trade out and offering them the alternative to open it again for a new contract month and at the new contract price.

Regular Closeout

The regular closeout is the most typical form of closeout. The futures position is closed by the trader at the existing market price. A regular closeout is used by traders for most of the time, and they usually do not hold positions for the long term till the expiry of the futures.

Different Types of Futures Contracts and Codes

It is possible to technically develop a futures contract for anything. Two distinct counterparties are fundamentally required to establish the transaction. They do not essentially have to take place by carrying out exchange. Those futures should be traded that an official exchange has actually facilitated and standardized. As futures are a standardized control, they have a particular symbol structure and abbreviations. Trading of futures contract can take place in the markets listed below:

- Agricultural
- Currencies
- Equity Index
- Financial
- Meats/Dairy
- Metals
- Softs

A few of the future codes and abbreviations that may be used over the trading platform should be noted. It is vital to be aware of what these are, it is vital to monitor your margin and what contracts month is being traded. The abbreviations for every contract month are listed below:

- F= January
- G= February
- H = March
- J= April
- K=May
- M=June
- N=July
- Q= August
- U=September
- V= October
- Z= December

For example, if you want to see what the current price of Natural Gas futures is for a given month (January) and year (2016), you will have to look for the symbol code NGF6.

NG stands for Natural Gas; F refers to the present contract month and 6 refer to the final digit of the expiration year, i.e. 2016.

It is significant to get to know how contracts function before one becomes involved in their trading. In addition, starting to trade the futures contracts, their expiry date should be known. The risk of futures contracts is quite high; however, it may be the most rapid and liquid instrument that is traded. There is high liquidity, low spread and predictable volatility of futures contracts.

HOW TO TRADE FUTURES?

Stop-loss orders are the more secure means of trading a futures contract. These orders are basically instructions that stop the damage at a fixed level. In addition, they may also lock in profits; hence, investors would benefit from having stop-loss orders.

Stop-loss orders are placed at the point when trade commences. For example, with respect to frozen concentrated orange juice contracts, the sale price of Dan Aykroyd was $1.42. Eventually, the price would decrease to 29 cents. This would cause significant damages to anyone purchasing these contracts, just like the damage caused to Ralph Bellamy and Don Ameche. However, if they had purchased Aykroyd's contract with a stop-loss order of $1.40, they would have been automatically removed from the position when the price dropped lower than $1.40. This would have decreased the substantial amount of loss they incurred otherwise.

In contrast, when the price increased to $1.50, Bellamy and Ameche could have modified their actual stop-order from $1.40 to $1.48 to make sure that they achieve profits of at least eight cents in case the price of concentrated orange juice starts decreasing again.

When people look at secure investments, they frequently have to pay a price for it. For example, continuing with the example of stop-order at $1.40, a situation may arise when the price dropped for a little while to $1.38 and then quickly increased to more than $1.50. These profits will not be added to your bank account as your contract ends automatically at the instant your price touches the stop-loss order limit.

A stop-loss order should not be cancelled after it has been placed. You were the one who started the order, possibly as part of a comprehensive investment strategy, and it would not be a good idea to cancel it as an emotional response to events that take place subsequently. Also, do not change your position in a market without sensible and logical reasons. If you like to work in the absence of a net, you can work without stop-loss orders. However, you should realize that this creates the chance of losing a greater amount of money than what you have in your bank account.

A stop-loss order is important because of the margin call. As you invest a small proportion of the contract value, it is vital to have a minimum amount of cash in your account, which is known as the maintenance margin. When the price of the commodity goes below that level, a margin call is made so that you can increase the amount of money in your account up to its initial level. When a margin call is made, you should instantly pay. If you do not do so, the brokerage is capable of liquidating your overall position to meet the losses. This is the reason why so many people gave up their lives when the stock market tumbled in 1929.

Similar to your overall investment portfolio, a significant part can be played by diversity in decreasing the risk inherent in trading futures. The most successful traders across the globe restrict their investment in a single commodity to a maximum of 3 to 5% of their trading capital. This is what your approach should also be. You should create your positions in as many markets as possible, for example, in gold, corn, crude oil as well as the Nasdaq. However, you should make sure that you avoid entering a market without reasons to back your investment. That is, do not attempt to develop a diversified futures portfolio just for the sake of diversity.

When you are looking for new markets to develop a portfolio, you should see further than the large exchanges, such as the Chicago Board of Trade or the Chicago Mercantile Exchange, and other exchanges where it is possible to take up significantly small-scale contracts (up to 80% smaller). This would make it easier for you to enter into various commodities. You can also participate in paper trading (using of imaginary trades and adopting real-market outcomes for a given time period), if you believe that this approach of acquiring information about new investments is useful. However, this approach is not similar to trading with actual money.

DIFFERENT TYPES OF SECURITIES

Different kinds of securities are present in the market. Security is described in finance as a financial asset that can be traded. This suggests that buying and selling of the financial asset can take place in financial markets.

SECURITIES ARE financial instruments that are developed to offer various alternatives to the investors. The owner of a financial instrument can buy, sell, hold, take up or give away their ownership. Hence, securities play a vital part in the international financial system.

Some securities are traded more often as compared to their counterparts. Preference is given by day traders to some securities, such as currencies, stocks and contracts for difference. Some other kinds of future contracts are currency futures, commodity futures, equity index futures and interest rate futures.

Securities are basically the financial instruments traded on exchanges all over the world. A few of the well-established exchanges known for the trade of securities are New York Stock

Exchange, London Stock Exchange, as well as those in Tokyo, Hong Kong, Sydney, Paris, etc.

There are a few securities, like bonds and other fixed-income assets that are traded throughout the secondary markets. Different securities, including bonds and stocks, are held by millions of investors across the globe. Exchange-traded funds or ETFs and mutual funds are other entities.

The public can access a security after it has been vetted. The regulator has to examine big firms and corporations that want to get listed at the stock market to collect funds for various objectives. The SEC or Securities Exchange Commission is the regulating body in the US. The bonds and stock markets are also called capital markets. Those companies that want to collect funds from the public get listed on the markets so that individuals and institutions can buy their stocks and carry out their trading whenever needed.

It is imperative for large companies to liaise with investment bankers and underwriters to facilitate them in getting their securities listed in the market. They may consist of stocks, bonds, etc. The company's financial position will usually be evaluated by the investment bankers, as well as the amount it wishes to collect. On this basis, the investment banker may suggest the number of issues and securities that are to be issued and how the overall listing process can be carried out.

The most well-known and widely available kinds of financial securities are stocks and bonds. In addition, they are the securities that are traded most often. In addition to these, some other financial instruments are traded in the capital markets, such as currencies, options, derivatives, indexes, debentures, warrants, as well as US Treasury securities.

There are a few common features in all these securities. All of them have a specific value that makes them attractive for traders as well as investors, which is why they trade these securities in the markets. Each of these securities has a different risk profile. Since there is distinct risk appetite of the different investors and traders, they make different decisions regarding the securities to trade or invest in.

For example, consider stocks and bonds. In comparison to bonds, the risk level of stocks is higher because of the way they react to changes in the market and the overall state of the economy. The stability of bonds is higher, though they offer a fixed income.

Stocks

By far, stocks are the most widely exchanged form of security for both investors as well as traders in the market. Different types of stock exist in the market, for example ordinary shares, which the parent company sells to the public in the stock market. Stocks of the highly successful firms that have been making profits for several years are known as blue-chip stocks. Internal stocks and niche-specific stocks are also traded in the market. Those common stocks that are traded frequently at exchanges are also referred to as equities. The widespread popularity of the stocks is because they offer the greatest return. The mean return provided by the stocks is 9.2%. Bonds, in contrast, have shown a return of around 6.5% in the same period spanning across 50 years.

Bonds

Bonds are another widely traded form of security among day traders. Bonds are essentially the kind of investment in which money is put in either public or private debt by the investors. Hence, bonds are mainly regarded as debt instruments.

Bonds are additionally referred to as debt securities; hence, a debt instrument is being bought by a trader dealing in bonds. In contrast, a trader dealing in stocks is actually dealing with the ownership units of a listed firm.

The objective of companies or firms issuing bonds is mainly to raise money for a particular financial obligation. For example, a bond may be issued by governments to extend or enhance the local infrastructure, whereas companies issue bonds to enter into new markets or to establish a new product line and related ventures.

Instruments that are similar to bonds are also issued by banks, which are called certificates of deposit. These are issued by banks to collect the money required to give loans to customers. A specific fixed rate of interest is usually provided to investors or buyers of these certificates. Certificates of deposits are basically short-term investment instruments that bank use to collect money for their operations.

Options and Derivatives

A derivative is another popular kind of security. Derivatives are basically financial securities, and their values have a direct link with an underlying security. This indicates that the price is derived from that of the underlying asset, which is why it is known as a derivative.

An options contract is an appropriate example of derivatives. Equity options contract refer to contracts established between buyers and sellers with respect to an underlying asset. Most of the times, these assets are stocks. Options are not traded by many retail traders; however, a large number of professional traders are there who frequently carry out options trading. In addition, investment companies, commercial and investment banks, hedge funds and other companies also trade in options contract when they want to create a balanced portfolio.

Equity options are, at the basic level, contracts that offer a right to the buyers to buy or purchase underlying stocks at a given price and within a specified time period. It should be noted that this is a right and not an obligation. In contrast, it is mandatory for the seller to sell when the buyer uses his right. Derivatives are very risky, and so those who have just started trading should avoid dealing in derivatives.

Currencies

Often, trade-in currencies are known as Forex or foreign exchange, in which currencies are bought or sold through an exchange. Currency trading is carried out with the aim of making a profit. The logic prevalent in currency trading is that there are persistent fluctuations in currency prices and traders can capitalize on these fluctuations to generate a profit.

Currency trading is preferred by certain day traders because the currency market is the biggest market all over the world. It achieves a turnover of $2 trillion every single day. This is a huge amount in comparison to the other big security markets, for example the NYSE.

3

WHAT AND WHERE TO TRADE?

Futures contracts include nearly all the commodities that are used by individuals in their routine lives and also the main investment areas, and these are traded at exchanges throughout the world.

There are various categories of futures markets, for example, metals, grains, energies, interest rates, stock indexes, currencies, and so on. One can choose the particular commodities, contract sizes and time periods for trading.

There are many important factors that need to be taken into account before one starts trading. These are in addition to the trend and trade establishments and are discussed below.

Margins:

Before you start taking part in trading activities, you will have to pay a margin to the exchanges as your insurance that the contract conditions will be fulfilled. There can be significant differences in the size of margins for different commodity contracts. For instance, the margin for an index contract, such as the S&P 500 can be quite high ($25,000), while that of the grain contracts can be quite low ($400). The size of the contract and the instability of the commodity determine the margin. You should make sure that you have sufficient cash in your trading account that can cover your margin. If profits are made on your contract position, you will get your margin back, in addition to the profit. However, if it is making a loss and the loss amount is greater than what is available in your trading account, your broker will call you and ask you to add more funds to your account as soon as possible to sustain your position. This is known as a margin call.

Volume:

The volume of the contract should be checked before you become involved in a trade. Volume refers to the number of contracts that are traded every day. The volume for a given day can be determined by adding just the amount of long contracts for a day, while leaving out the short contracts. The future market is known as a net sum zero game, which means that for each winning trade, you have a losing trade, and for every trade, there is someone who is buying and someone who is selling a contract. Those markets that have high volume offer you the opportunity to enter and leave a trade at your desired levels. However, when there is very little volume, there may be no party on the other side to take your trade. This indicates that there are chances that your orders will be poorly executed.

Open Interest:

This refers to the number of contracts that are still open at the closing of each day. It also serves as a good example of the liquidity of the market. When open interest is low, there is low trading interest and there is high possibility of bad "fills".

Volatility:

When a specific commodity has a highly volatile price, which quickly shifts across an extensive range each day, it may be possible that your trading account gets empty rapidly, even if you have made the right predictions about the long-run trend. It is important for you to examine the volatility of a commodity in the past before taking the decision to trade so that you can determine if the volatility is appropriate for your risk profile. There may be high open interest and volume of certain commodities; however, it may be implied that you should restrict your trade to other commodities that exhibit low volatility. This means that you should carry out trade of commodities whose everyday trading range is narrow.

4

———

PRINCIPLES OF FUTURES TRADING

One of the most commonly asked question with respect to futures trading is what really happens when one purchases futures? This can be answered in a single sentence: when you purchase futures, you are actually giving your agreement to purchase products or services that has not yet been created by the company from whom you purchased these futures.

The risk inherent in futures trading is quite high as compared to stock trading as you are dealing with products or services that have not yet been created. These features make future trading quite popular, not just among the producing firms, individuals and customers, but also among the speculators.

The trading of stocks or shares takes place on stock markets, while futures are traded on futures markets. The concept of futures market emerged as an outcome of the needs of agricultural producers in the mid-nineteenth century, where the demand was frequently quite higher than the supply.

In the present times, futures market have extended the borders of agricultural production and become part of various other fields, such as the financial domain. Hence, futures markets are used presently for the buying and selling of currencies and of few other financial instruments. Futures markets provide opportunity to a farmer to take part in the exchange of goods with customers in other parts of the globe. The International Monetary Market (IMM) that was created in 1972 is one of the largest and most important futures markets.

Futures represent financial derivatives and their value is determined by the changes in the price of another asset. This suggests that the price of futures is not determined by its inherent value; rather, it depends on the price of the asset that is being tracked by the futures contract.

A key benefit of the futures market is that it is centralized and that people from all parts of the globe can create futures contracts electronically. The price of the merchandize will be determined by these futures contract, as well as the time of delivery. In addition, important information is included in each futures contract regarding the quantity and quality of the goods sold, the specified price and ways in which the goods will be transferred to the buyers.

The overall worth of the contract is not paid by the individual who has bought or sold a futures contract. Rather, he pays a small percentage as a fee to take up an open position. For instance, if the futures contract has a value of $350,000 and the S&P 500 is 1400, then the initial margin payment that he makes is just $21,875. This margin is established by the exchange and may be modified at any point in time.

When the S&P increases to 1500, the value of the futures contract is going to be $375,000. Therefore, the individual will attain a profit of $25,000. But if the index decreased to 1390 from the initial level of 1400, then he will face a loss of $2,500 as the value of the futures contract will now be $347,500. This loss of $2,500 has not yet been realized. The individual will not have to add more cash to his trading account.

When the index decreases to 1300, the value of the futures contract will be $325,000. A loss of $50,000 will be experienced by the individual. The broker will ask him to add more cash to his trading account because the initial margin of $21,875 is not sufficient to cover the deficits.

Futures Market Categories

All future contracts have a few similarities. However, distinct assets may be tracked by each contract. Hence, it is vital to assess the different markets.

- **Agriculture**
- Grains
- Livestock
- Dairy
- Forest
- **Energy**
- Crude Oil
- Heating oil
- Natural gas
- Coal
- **Stock Index**
- S&P 500
- Nasdaq 100
- Nikkei 225
- E-mini S&P 500
- **Foreign Currency**
- Euro/USD
- GBP/USD
- Yen/USD
- Euro/Yen
- **Interest Rates**

- Treasuries
- Money markets
- Interest Rate Swaps
- Barclays Aggregate Index
- **Metals**
- Gold
- Silver
- Platinum
- Base Metals

FUTURES CONTRACTS CAN BE TRADED on various assets and categories. However, for a new trader, it is important to trade those assets that they are aware of. For instance, if you have been involved in stock trading for some time, you should use stock indexes at the start of your futures contract trading. This would make it easier for you to comprehend the underlying asset. You just need to comprehend the working of the futures market.

Once you have selected your category, you should determine which asset to trade. For instance, after choosing the energy category for trading futures contracts, you may decide to focus on natural gas, coal, heating oil or crude oil. Market trading takes place at different levels; hence, you should be aware of different things, such as market requirements, liquidity, contract sizes and volatility. Before trading in futures contracts, it is important to research on the important aspects.

Types of Trade

Through a basis trade, one can go long or short on a futures contract and short or long in the cash market. There are going to be fluctuations in the price difference between the two markets.

For instance, if you wish to purchase a 10-year US Treasury futures bond, then you should sell a physical 10-year US Treasury bond.

Through a spread trade, you can go short and long on two futures contracts. There will be variations in the price difference between the futures contracts. For instance, you may purchase an S&P 500 futures contract for delivery in August, while selling an S&P 500 futures contract for delivery in November.

In hedging trading, a futures contract is sold to balance your current position in the market. For instance, a stock trader may not be willing to sell his shares to evade taxes. However, because of the fear that the stock market may experience a severe dip, he sells S&P 500 futures contract in the form of a hedge.

A significant issue with respect to futures and future contracts is that of prices and limitations of futures contracts. Prices are denoted in future contracts as traditional currencies, like US dollars. In terms of futures contract, there is a least amount of money for which the product price may rise or decline. In terms of futures contracts, this minimum amount is known as "ticks".

Investors making investments worth a large amount of money or those purchasing significant number of products are influenced by these tricks as price fluctuations can have a huge impact on the money spent on particular products. These "ticks" vary for different merchandise. The "ticks" of each commodity being traded in the futures and the minimum price fluctuation for each is distinct, depending on its kind.

5

FUTURES SPREAD TRADING

ajority of the day traders give preference to futures over options as they have the surety of moving with their underlying asset. In addition, it is possible to evaluate the futures market directly, which suggests that you may benefit from market predictions, without considering derivative pricing.

In addition, in contrast to a few markets, no artificial limits exist that prevent you from short trading, because of which you are able to work as a day trader more efficiently. Lastly, FINRA's description of a pattern day trader is not applicable. One of the requirements of a pattern day trader is to always have cash of $25,000. In addition, once you are labeled as one, trading becomes a more challenging job for you.

Adherence to Trends:

It is important for you to consistently adhere to the trends. It is likely that being drawn towards futures trading, your inclination to follow market trends is less as you would rather wish to capitalize on the opportunities that are emerging. You will have to break this habit if you plan to carry out futures trading as you will eventually discover that there is significantly higher profitability of this approach of adhering to the trends of the key players and showing as little deviation as possible from them.

Don't Prioritize Trade Frequency:

Another important point is to avoid giving priority to trade frequency. It is natural for day traders to trade more than other kinds of traders; however, this does not mean that one should be carrying out futures trade all the time. You should always remember that one can be successful as a day trader by making three trades a day in the same way as the day trader who makes 30 trades each day. The key point here is to select future targets carefully and clearly comprehend the direction in which all trades are moving. You should always carry out a complete risk/reward assessment before confirming any trade to make sure that it is worthwhile in the long term.

Know What Good Futures Contract Looks Like:

You should be aware of what a good futures contract is. Before commencing any trade, you should obtain as much information as possible to make sure that you do not come across any unexpected situations. A significant point to note is that there may be several significant differences between futures contracts that need to be taken into account before moving ahead. You should be aware of the particular contract unit because each prospective futures contract will depict the size and the units it is trading in.

A specific currency will always be used to denote forex futures, whereas those that depend on stock indices usually consist of a reference point on the index multiplied by a given price per share. The details of this measurement are usually not very significant as they are only critical at the moment to enable you to comprehend precisely what you are becoming involved in.

Apart from these kinds of specifics, you should know about the quoted price and how this quote may vary among markets, because they may either be written in dollars and cents, or in the form of mathematical equations, percentages or probability points. The final outcome is always going to turn out to be the same; however, you should be aware of precisely what you are working with before you go ahead with it.

Choosing Right Contract:

You should ensure that you choose the correct contract. Before selecting the appropriate contracts, you should comprehend the different degrees of insecurity that are occurring within the market in comparison to the possibility of a serious payout in case everything works out well. This is important because there is significantly higher variance in the futures market compared to other markets because on the whole, they include much higher variety. When such kinds of decisions are to be made, a significant point to note is that in this case, the previous results are not going to accurately forecast the future outcomes. This indicates that even though price has stayed constant for many days, it is not necessary that it will remain so in the future.

Look for Right Signals:

You need to determine the correct signals. When carrying out day trading of futures, you should remember that you will be able to achieve best outcomes when you use three indicators that do not particularly have a link with each other. You should observe the sine wave as a way of identifying the price with respect to resistance and support, the momentum to identify the volume in comparison to the supply and the pro-am to identify the particular trade size, which will help you find out the degree to which the market is interested in the trade at that point in time.

You are generally expected to be capable of plotting the sine wave over the least chart pane so as to obtain a value of the existing cycle. When both the levels of support and resistance are determined, you may be able to observe the momentum plotted beneath the bars, which shows the price. It will subsequently be denoted by waves so as to depict the volume with respect to buying and selling.

You may also come across distinct divergence patterns that can be directly plotted over different additional price bars. When observing the pro-am, you may be able to easily take into account the different kinds of active traders that are trading at different price points. When you determine various highs, then it suggests that various position switching are occurring towards the top-end of the spectrum. On the other hand, a large number of lows suggest that the breakout is in its final stages, indicating that it may reverse at any point.

Consider Direction Trend is Forming:

Take into account the direction of the trend: in more conventional types of trading, if you identify a trend while carrying out day trading, then it is highly likely that you are going to successfully generate profits from it, presuming it stays that way for a sufficient amount of time. With respect to determining the direction of a possible trend, you may want to identify professionals who are trading in the field before making sure that the trend is going to keep on moving ahead. You may want keep track of indicators that it has attained a point where its volume is consumed, which suggests that it is possibly in its final stages.

Continue Operating in Single Market:

Though there are several sub-divisions of futures market that pertain to distinct markets, you should not switch from one market to another as you have greater chances of achieving success when you stick to the markets that have offered success in the initial stages. After becoming an expert in a particular subdivision of the market, you can move over to another market. However, till that time, you should concentrate on how you can enhance success in the long run.

Futures Spreads Trading Pricing and Margins

Spreads:

It is important to remember that there will be a reduction in the individual margins on a contract provided they belong to a spread. For instance, on a provided wheat contract, the margin is $2000 but it will become as low as $200 if you opt to go both short and long on wheat in a single year. However, this margin can double to $400 if you decide to go short and long on a single product spread over various years. If the volatility of the spread is smaller as compared to that in the given contract, the price differential shows up.

Often, you are enabled to observe market movement very closely through the future spread. Hence, both contracts will be influenced if anything big occurred in the wheat market; however, the music of the increased risk will be largely faced by the singular contract as compared to the other.

Price Concerns:

The supposed difference between two contracts helps in determining the price of a certain futures spread. Simply, subtracting the next month from the price of the front month is the easiest method to accurately determine the spread's pricing. The spread becomes positive if the price of the front-month is higher than the other one and the spread is negative if it is lower. There will be no change in the values of both the contracts and the spreads. For instance, the spread will be assumed to be -$10 if $500 is the price of the wheat in the front month and $510 in the following, however it would be $10 if it decreased to $490.

Market Types

Contango Markets:

If it is apparent that the cost will be lower in the front month as compared to the deferred month, the market is believed to be contango. Usually, it indicates that the cost in the subsequent month will be a little higher than the front month owing to the cost to carry.

The operating costs along with other associated costs of storage or insurance of the location where the concerned product is actually sold require capital which comes with an interest rate that which will be considered by the cost to carry.

Backward Markets:

If the front months have a greater value than the subsequent months, the market is thought to be surrounded by backwardation. It is also called as inverted market which is contradictory to the standard market condition. It often happens when the market is going through a bull phase which is a result of supply chain issue, which is usually associated to a considerable rise in demand while the overall supply is limited. When a full brunt of the change is experienced by the front months, this kind of price differential takes place generally which is then forwarded to the upcoming months. This condition often occurs when the subsequent month falls in the subsequent crop year followed by the front month.

Keeping the condition of the market aside, it is significant that the seasonal factors should always be considered while making the choices. Usually, it can be predicted that in summer, the prices of gasoline will be higher whereas in winters the prices of natural gas, coffee and heating oil increases. Moreover, you should always keep in mind that markets predictably undergo bearish and bullish periods however, the influence tends to be not much consistent on the commodities overall.

Common Spread Types:

Inter-Commodity Futures:

contracts are included in these futures which are spread throughout different markets. For instance, you will be selling corn and buying wheat, if you think that high demand for wheat will be triggered in the market than corn. If the corn prices remain lower than the wheat prices, then the individual prices for every product does not impact.

Calendar Intra-Commodity:

A single commodity between various months of the year is taken into account by this spread. For instance, you would prefer to go long in November and short in June if you assume that the November will be marked as a strong month for the wheat market as compared to June. If the prices are on the rise in November as compared to June, then the specifics of the price does not influence.

Bull Futures:

A single commodity is considered by this spread assuming that higher price will be triggered in the front month as compared to the next month. For instance, you will wish that the price is higher in May as compared to the selling month of June if you have bought a bullish wheat future in May. It is significant to remember for this kind of future that the upcoming future contracts have a tendency to proceed speedily as you move away from the front month from where the name of the bull future is derived. The individual is a bullish trader who purchases in the front month believing that it will begin to proceed at a higher rate as compared to the subsequent month.

Bear Futures:

If you purchase the similar commodity in a manner that you go long on the following month while you go short in the front month, this spread takes place. For instance, you will wish that the prices are low in May as compared to in June, if you buy wheat in

May with the intention to sell it in June. It is significant to remember for this kind of future that deferred future contracts are inclined to move speedily as you move away from the front month from where the name of this future has been derived. You should look forward to buy this kind of spread if you are sure that prices will not rise.

6

HOW CAN WE MAKE PROFIT ON FUTURES MARKETS?

An important thing to keep in mind is regardless of your purchase and selling of future contracts in commodities, the delivery is typically not undertaken by you. The contracts have to be closed prior to the date of delivery.

Let's assume an example and associate it to a futures contract. You came across a house that is put up for sale in $300 000. You are of the opinion that its value will rise by around 10% in the upcoming year but you kept down a $30 000 deposit because unfortunately, you does not have sufficient money to purchase the house right away. As per expectation, the value of the property increased after a year by 10% and is now valued at $330 000. You choose to sell the property which will yield you a profit of $30 000. Your profit on your investment is 100% because initially, you invested $30 000 and sold it with a $30 000 profit.

The function of commodity trading is quite similar. For instance, you have done analysis of the corn market and you assume that the prices will rise, thus you choose to purchase the September contract which is currently trading at $2.40 per bushel.

A corn contract has 5000 bushels. A $500 deposit or margin is paid by you as needed by the exchange.

As per the expectations, the price rose to $3.40 a bushel after four weeks. Thus, $3.40 X 5000 = $17000 is the value of the contract now. You earned a profit of $5000 ($17000 -$12000) on the contract which you purchased four weeks ago at $12000 ($2.40 X 5000). $5000 is the return on your investment of $500 which is 10% in only 4 weeks.

The profits can also be made while the market is facing a drop in prices. For example, you assume the prices of soybeans will drop from its present point of $5.00 per bushel. In a soybean contract, there are 5000 bushels too. You sold one September contract at the present level. A $1000 deposit or margin is paid by you. As per expectations, a significant drop in the prices was experienced after six weeks to $3.50 per bushel. Now your decision is to avail your profits and shut your position. Your purchase of the contract enabled you to balance the contract which was sold six weeks ago. Your profit is the difference between the price you sold and the price you purchased back. On an investment of $1000, $25000($5.00 X 5000) – $17500($3.5 X 5000) = $7500 is the profit. This means a profit of 7.5% in six weeks.

Selling Short - How Does it Work?

In a dropping state of the market, how can an individual earn money? This thing occurs in a routine in our lives. For example, you deal in cars and sell zero meter cars. You got a supply from the factory of two cars on consignment that you will showcase the cars on the showroom floor and the factory does not demand for money straight away as it is providing you time to sell them. One of the cars was sold for $50 000 after some time and now it's the time to pay $30 000 to the factory, thus $20 000 is your profit. What is done by you actually? The car you bought from the factory was sold by you at a greater price than the actual factory price and hence you earned money. You purchased it after selling it. This is what we do when we sell futures. As we assume that the market will experience a drop in prices we sell high and then we can either buy it again or close our position at a cheaper price and make money like the car dealer.

There Must Be Risks

Risks are associated with every business. A big amount of capital is needed to be invested when you start a business. Before the customer comes up, you have to purchase stock, give salaries, pay rent, etc. You will be clueless about the number of customers walking in and that whether you will be able to create enough profits that will recover your investment. It is the same with an assumed market; however, your success will be dependent upon your risk management skill.

Let's draw a contrast between the futures market and the stock market. Your risk can be diversified in the stock market through investment in various non-correlated stocks and under general conditions, it will go well; however, unexpected political changes or news about the economy can influence the share prices within a night. In extreme conditions, your entire profits can be washed away, no matter how many companies your investments are spread in just as we have observed in current years. On the other hand, in futures market, your investments are spread throughout a big variety of commodity markets such as oil, wheat, corn, cotton, sugar or silver. Hence, no circumstances can influence all of these markets at the same time. Nevertheless, political events, floods, drought, war and economic disasters cannot be escaped and they do influence specific commodity markets, but your risk reduces through spreading of investment while your losses reduce and you are capable to take advantage from any price move, either up or down. For instance, if the wheat crop is hit by an unexpected flood which created shortages and hence the price increases or maybe the prices drop owing to the bumper crop, still you are in a position to take advantage from both prices moving up or down. Both upwards and downwards trends are observed by the commodity traders.

This ability enables you to diversify your investment throughout various uncorrelated markets and earn huge profits on short term investments within some weeks which will lead to more interest in futures trading as the risk factor is less as compared to the stock market.

Trading Like Professionals

Who is the most successful in generating profits in any industry? They are the professionals. It is because they do a lot of relevant research, train themselves accordingly and strictly follow the rules of their trading systems and don't believe in shortcuts. As an example, consider what can happen if doctors believe that the techniques they have learned back in university are useless and start testing their own techniques during an operation of which they have no prior experience? In my opinion, we will start losing trust on them and will not let them test on us as we are uncertain about the result. We put our trust in the medical procedures because we are very sure that doctors are well trained and well-disciplined professionals and know their job and will give treatment according to the given conditions and will not opt for shortcuts.

You must be thinking what is the connection of a doctor with a commodity trading? For becoming a successful commodity trader, you should behave like a professional and never compromise on your rules of trading system and don't ever go for shortcuts.

Undoubtedly, most of the commodity traders (nearly 80% of

them) experience losses. This is quite a disturbing fact, however, the majority of the losers are gamblers and their loss in any business is at high probability. Fear or greed is their motivating factor and thus they are unaware of ethics and discipline of trading systems and take high risks.

Now there is a clear picture of the reason behind so many people making losses thus don't ever attempt such acts. This manual will make you aware of the mistakes made by other people so that you can avoid them as well as will make you capable to stand amongst those 20% who exceptionally earn money.

Trading Methods

Fundamentally, the trading methods are of two types:

Fundamental Trading

In this part you have to do research on the markets where you wish to trade; weather conditions reported by daily press should be read thoroughly and daily, information like supply and demand figures should be studied as well as economic news and agricultural reports, etc. Huge amount of time and money are needed to be invested by big institutional investors with the required resources to perform all the research.

Technical Trading

This method is also called Technical Analysis and it is based on drawing charts to assess the trend of the markets. It is the best method for small traders. A lot of subjective information is not necessary for making decisions.

Technical Analysis

The technical analysis is an interesting activity which allows you to learn about the basic concepts of charting and makes you learn to time your trades with accuracy.

What is Technical Analysis?

Price action will be studied here by using charts with an aim of classifying price trends. The identification of the direction of the trend in the long-term and to utilize it to get financial edge is the main aim of price action.

Who Uses Technical Analysis?

The users of technical analysis include Entrepreneurs who aim for making fortunes, Professional fund managers who earn their living by offering expert investment advice to other people and also used by hedgers who are the owner of the physical commodities. In a nutshell, every market participant who needs a professional advantage uses technical analysis. One thing is explained by it that technical analysis is very important as it is used by the professionals. Before expecting good results, we must realize the importance of technical analysis.

7

CANDLESTICKS

The technical tools that collect data from multiple time frames and incorporate it into single price bars are called candlestick charts and they are very useful as compared to the conventional Open High, Low Close Bars also known as OHLC which in other words are only basic simple lines which join the dots of closing prices. After accomplishment, the patterns constructed by candlesticks are efficient enough to fore-tell direction of the price. This colorful technical tool is further elaborated through proper color coding. This tool existed even in the 18th century when it was used by rice traders.

Day traders use candlestick charts as it enables them to see the image of price movements at its best by showing the open, high, low, and close values in terms of up or down sessions. The candle-stick patterns are of various kinds and there is a variety of candle-stick formations which are created off price actions to facilitate traders with a forecast of the upcoming events. Other chart types can also implement these formations which consist of point and figure charts, box plot, box charts, etc.

Price Action and Mass Psychology

The movement of a security's price which is constructed over a time period is termed as price action. It is the fundamental pillar of all the technical analysis regarding a commodity, an asset chart or a stock. Price action turned out to be highly reliable for most of the short-term traders like day traders as it consists of every formation and trend which is deduced from it to help in taking trade decisions. Price action develops the practice of technical analysis as past are integrated in it while calculating which helps to add more information in trading decisions. When using the charts to construct prices over a time span, it can be observed and analyzed. Various chart compositions are used by the traders to increase their capability of identifying and analyzing breakouts, trends and reversals.

Usually, price action is not regarded as a tool for trading such as an indicator. Rather, it is considered as a data source which is the basis of creation of tools. Price action is closely associated with swing traders and trend traders which eliminate any basic assessment for only paying attention to either support level and/ or resistance level to forecast association and breakouts. Other factors apart from current price should also be focused by the traders like the volume of trading and the periods employed by them to create levels.

Moreover, trading is influenced by psychology. A significant part of human life is psychology and it affects humans as a whole in their interaction with events and experiences which happens in a routine. Psychology is crucial in day trading as well because only price changes or other market factors are not solely responsible for impacting the decisions of investors and traders. The success and failure of the trader also depend on psychological factors such as mass psychology. The definition for mass psychology could be the actions and decisions taken by the traders while keeping in mind the news, emotions and other resources. It involves adhering to market trends and convictions. The data regarding facts and figures of the market where they are aiming to invest in is used by the traders. Consequently, market is inclined towards imitating the average trends. In the market, everyone imitates each other owing to the psychological makeup of the people and hence it generates conventional judgment. The downside of this is that humans are likely to make mistakes anyhow, which as a result influences financial market, leaving it inefficient to some extent.

Candlestick Charts

Bullish candlesticks are of various kinds: bullish engulfing, bullish harami, and hammer.

A green candle with a big body is the bullish engulfing candlestick, which covers a complete range of the previous red candle. The reversal becomes sharper in this candlestick as the body is huge. Nevertheless, the previous red candle body should be fully covered by the body.

The very efficient bullish engulfing candlesticks are generated by the tail end of a downtrend which generated an extreme reversal bounce which engulfs short sellers, creating a panic short-covering buying agitation. The bargain hunters are hence encouraged by this, to leave the boundary and go beyond through increasing the pressure of buying. The expected reversals on downtrends are signaled by this kind of candle while it also gives a continuation signal for uptrend when they occur following the reversion pullbacks. The bullish engulfing candles become very efficient when the volume is anticipated to increase by double of the average. The next candlestick is formed by the buy triggers which permits the high of the bullish engulfing candlestick.

A backward version of the bearish engulfing candlestick pattern is developed by the bullish harami candlestick where the smaller harami candle is surpassed by a big body engulfing candle. It is expected that the previous engulfing red candle will form a capitulation large body candlestick which created the lowest low point of the sequence displaying a capitulation sell-off, which occurs before the harami candle which is falling under the range of the engulfing candle and is likely to be trading better. The short-sellers remain in the state of complacency due to the subtleness of the small body as in their opinion the stocks will go down again, but they rather stabilized before they can develop a reversal bounce which happens to be a surprise for the short seller as the stock reverses to the highest. This kind of candlestick is an efficient indicator that makes sellers to remain satisfied till the trend reverses gradually. Nevertheless, in contrast to bullish engulfing it is not much nerve-racking or intense. Hence, its subtleness makes it very dangerous for short-sellers as the process of is quite slow but it rises swiftly. The buy long trigger is created when the next candle increases through the high of the previous engulfing candle, then breaks can be plotted underneath the lows of the harami candle.

Lastly, the bullish reversal candlestick consist of the hammer candlestick type and it stands amongst the most used candlestick patterns which is employed to develop the capitulation bottoms and after that a price bounce is used by the traders to integrate into long positions. This kind of candlestick usually develops at the end of a downtrend to highlight an immediate term price bottom. There is a lower shadow in the hammer candle which develops a new low in the downtrend pattern and closes back up close to or above the open as well. Nonetheless, the lower shadow also called the tail is assumed to become minimum two or even greater times the size of the body. When the positions are being covered by the shorts and bargain hunters come to a decision, it shows the longs who had surrendered in the end. A rise in volume solidifies the hammer. Thus, it is significant for approving the hammer candle that the candles that follows closes higher than the low of the hammer candle or it should close above the body as recommended. The typical buy signal is an entry that is higher than the high of the hammer with a long trail stop positioned below the body of the low of the hammer candle. Timing an entry is a sensible decision employing a momentum indicator like the MACD, stochastic, or the RSI.

There are various bearish candles too alike various kinds of bullish candles; namely; the shooting star, bearish engulfing, and the bearish harami.

The bearish reversal candlestick consists of the shooting star candlestick type and it signifies a peak or a top. It is the reverse version of the hammer candle. Conventionally, a minimum of three or even more following green candles are traced by this type of candlestick which signals the increasing price and demand. Moving further, the patience is lost by the buyers and they tend to run after the new price highs, which are contained in a pattern before they realize that they have paid more.

The upper shadow also called as a wick should normally be two times larger than the body size. This indicates that the entry of last buyer part of the frenzied buyer group has taken place at last in the stock as the positions are also closed by the profit-takers. After this, short sellers push the prices downward to close the candle close to or lower than the opening. This is done to trap the late buyers who intended to run after the high prices. Here, the fear heightens as the appropriate candle which follows is likely to be close to or below the shooting star candle and it triggers a panic selling spree because late buyers being satisfied want to close their position to overcome losses. Generally, when the low of the following candlestick breaks, the short sell signal forms, which indicates that trail stops are at the high of the body or at the tail of the candlestick.

A strong price reversal candlestick is the bearish engulfing candlestick. This is a kind of candlestick which eclipses the overall range of the previous green candlestick. Here, the body of the preceding green candle is entirely concealed in the candlestick body. The complete range of previous candlesticks is swallowed by some bodies in case of stronger bearish engulfing candlesticks which incorporates the upper as well as the lower shadows. Nevertheless, they could be pointing towards some gigantic selling activities on a panic reversal from bullish to bearish attitudes.

The buyers who employ previous green candles do not predict and remain positive owing to the fact that it should be trading close to the high of an uptrend. Longs gather hope for another leap from this kind of candlestick as it opens up higher and it signals more bullish attitudes at an early stage. Nevertheless, the sellers follow a stronger and sharper manner of pushing the prices down by the opening point. This is alarming for the longs. Selling increases continuously as it carries on to drop by the low of early close and it generates more panic selling as majority of the buyers from preceding sales window have now sunk with their shares. Selling continues to increase until the candle close as all the buyers from preceding close are now bearing losses.

The size of reversal is often quite sudden. The bearish engulfing candles are called reversal candles, when they develop on uptrend as they force the trend of more sales into closure. But the passing of low of the bullish engulfing candlestick results in the formation of the short-selling triggers. The formation of candlestick on the reverse bounce may be the reason behind downtrends as new buyers may stick on this leap.

The dealer must consider volumes for all candlestick patterns; however, special attention must be given to the engulfing candles. For being impactful, the volume must be more than twice of the regular trading volumes. Algorithms are well-known for drawing the tape with a mix tick to sell out fictional engulfing candles for which it is very easy to capture bears.

The vice versa of bearish harami candle is the bullish harami candle, where the collection of harami candle is overshadowed by the previous engulfing candle. As prior green candle forms a new high due to its bigger frame, engulfing candles form at the peak of the uptrend ahead of small harami candlestick being created because the force of purchasing eventually decreases. Because of the slow buying trend, the longs raise an assumption of pullbacks being just a break before continuing uptrend. First, the bearish harami candle shuts followed by closing lower of the next candle which is a state of worry for longs. The pause in the low of preceding engulfing candle creates panic sell-off and longs exit to prevent more deficit. When the low of engulfing candle is cracked, the traditional short sell is triggered and pauses or breaks may occur at the top of harami candle high.

Doji candlestick, which can also be called as indecision is another kind of candlestick which follows reversal design that can be bullish or bearish. The type of pattern depends on the purpose of the candle prior to it. The candle with protracted shadows usually has standardized open or close prices. It may have a miniature body though it resembles cross. Not only a Doji is called as symbol of indecision but it also acts as a line to specify limits. As it is mostly a reversal candle, the direction of candle can be a signal of premature indecisiveness of the turn that the reversal will take.

Before the formation of Doji, there are the preceding bulling candles. Out of these candles, the one that is next to the body low often sends a sell or short sell signs at the pauses of Doji candlestick lows with route being stopped at the top of Doji highs. In the situation when the preceding candles are bearish while Doji candlestick forms bullish reversal, the protracted triggers that are atop of the body or on candlestick high and one trail terminate at the low of the Doji. Every candlestick narrates a story of bulls and bears, the consumers and suppliers, the market demand and supply as well as personal traits like: dread or lust. The candle patterns need confirmation. This confirmation is derived on the basis of the preceding candles and the lines following them. The most common mistake of new businesses is that they only spot a single candle formation and fail to register the context that's why it is advised to always carefully understand what each candle shows and the message it transfers for the better understanding of the complexity and technicality of the candlestick chart patterns. These chart patterns can be repetitive but when the context is ignored the market does the same with dealers. More emotions and affects can be exhibited by coloring the bodies in candlestick patterns. Thus, involving them with other indicators in order to achieve better performance seems to be a great idea.

There is a little difference between hanging man candlestick and hammer candlestick which is that it forms at the top of uptrend rather than bottom of downtrend. This particular kind of candlestick has small frame and lower shadow but the shadow is big in comparison to body. It is desirable for lower shadow to be twice as big as or even bigger than the size of body. It also possesses a tiny upper shadow. The hanging candlestick is different from Doji as its body is formulated at the top of the series. Quite often the bullish feeling is sustained and maintained in this candlestick unnaturally as it fails to satisfy the buyer for some unknown reasons thus, the candle is raised closely to the upper range. However, the reality sets in as the candle closes below the hanging man followed by the increase in sales.

This type of candle is formed by combining more than four consecutive Doji candles which is most helpful when it reaches peak of price spikes resembling parabola. Hanging candlesticks are unpopular as they indicate the buyers who got stuck when they were in favor of momentum or attempting to achieve more liquidity to sell further by painting. The candlestick shows uptrend because the buyers after purchasing at high prices wonder why they bought on such a high price. The crack of the low of this candlestick triggers short sells as the trail is rested before the high of hanging candle.

The dark cloud cover candlestick, as the name suggests, is the reversal formation of three-candlestick where new highs of the upwards trend are made by the dark shadow cover candle resulting from a gap over the closing of the previous candle But it finally closes red due to early entry of sellers. This suggests that the longs were impatient to take a major action to sell their ranks even after formation of new highs. Dark cloud cover candle probably has bodies closing below the midpoint of preceding candlestick structure.

In the dark cloud candle, it is the three- candle pattern that is made up of previous candle and confirmation candle tracks it. A sequence of green candles is anticipated, in the preceding candlestick that will result in the dark cloud cover candlestick. The trading is prominent and the new buyers are tricked. If the candle that follows fails to achieve a new high means above the cloud cover candle, a short sell is triggered for the point where the low of third candlestick is distanced. This results in exposure of the trap door, showing panic selling as the longs start to leave the risk desperately trying to prevent losses. The short sell signal is activated when there is gap in the third candle's low through the trail signal stops that have been fixed above the candle. The difference between the dark cloud cover candlestick and the hanging man bearish is the shooting star and the Doji structure.

8

FUNDAMENTAL ANALYSIS

Fundamentals in Currencies Futures Market

It is crucial to understand an approach of differentiating between successful flourishing business and loss-making business in order to deal in markets in future fruitfully. This approach consists of two types of analysis that are: technical (explained below) and fundamental analysis. The difference between them is that fundamental analysis is much more in trend nowadays while technical analysis is the traditional one and regained popularity in last ten years. However, they work in distinct ways but the results are same and both are equally helpful. Fundamental analysis mainly determines information at bigger scale and for this reason it requires more time than technical analysis.

Further, this type of analysis depends on secondary information which increases the time span as this information is not readily available and after it comes in access it must be understood well to carry out the analysis effectively and efficiently. But, this allows evaluating quickly or predicting the likely conditions in future market with the help of large range of distinct components such as outlining general modulations in monetary policies of the countries we are concerned with. The final target is to gain enough data to identify the understated pair to which industry has not become familiar. So to design this kind of analysis, caution is the key to devise accurate results.

DETERMINE BASELINE:

Baseline must be considered before investing in other currencies to make this investment productive. The exchange rate is subject to constant fluctuations so it must be carefully analyzed. Baseline will help to determine the right time to invest in other currencies to maximize returns because it will not be difficult to identify the changes in the currency pair that justify the attention and thoughtfulness for it. Careful consideration will help business to take better decisions.

To decide a baseline, modernization of macroeconomic policies must be taken into account first as they will provide the bases of baseline and the information should not be incorrect or obsolete. To predict or foresee future situations, the history of the conduct will serve as an important and most trusted indicator. After having relevant knowledge about past, the present monetary situation should be considered also; it must be evaluated that for how long the currency will be on that stage as it is very unlikely for economy to stay on same stage.

An economic cycle that a currency follows consists of six different stages. Starting from the boom/peak phase, this is where the currency is highly geared up (that is large amounts of debts) and is quite stable. At the opposite side of this range there is a bust stage which has the features of lesser debt burden and alarming instability. The other stages include: post-bust, pre-bust, post-boom and pre-boom. This shows that each phase is following the other phase and these stages are inevitable. Identifying the current stage properly is a risky business as it is difficult to know whether we are doing the right thing to search a trading pair that will be successful and fruitful in the long-run as well.

The simplest method for identifying the current stage of the currency is to calculate the errors with bank loans and total reserves of the currency. When currency is enjoying boom period or it is near the corner, the numerical values are less. When post-boom phase reaches the numbers have stretched out. Consequently, if the particular numbers are greater than the baseline, then it can be concluded that bust phase has reached or is on its way.

The current stage of currency does not influence the amount of money that can be made. However, advantage of it can be taken before market follows as it will slow down the process.

The faster we are to identify the next stage, the better results will be expected (in form of higher dividends)

WORLDWIDE CONSIDERATIONS:

International economic trends must be identified once you comprehend the baseline, at which the currency pairs stay. It also must be analyzed that how these worldwide conditions will affect the exchange pairs. The symbols that will contribute to success once they become famous must be closely and carefully analyzed and investigated rather than just giving attention to evident indicators. In order to do so, the best approach is to research about technological advancements in associated countries as economies can be reversed in no time and conditions can change quickly.

Technological indicators provide an opportunity to fully utilize the stage of boom since by hitting the ground, the benefits can be reaped until the point where technology loses its charm and becomes common. The bust phase approaches as the currency reaches the point of saturation. People will take time in making decision of moving into markets based on expectations when the currency is either in the stage of post-bust or post-boom. The results are unpredictable and there are chances that this will affect negatively as the drift is always inevitable.

People will be satisfied with the little influence when it is known that the phase is going to be changed despite being sure of the exact time of phase change. In this scenario, people will be more content than in other phases as they will want to pay before any changes. On the contrast, when another phase is beginning then people will be willing to make deals even if it is more risky because at this point so much carefulness is not needed.

Global Implications:

The international monetary policies are very important in changing events and give an overview of the industry, though provincial or state concerns are also important. It is quite cumbersome to decide from where to start but firstly, the analysis that was designed at micro level must be implied on macro level. To start effectively, the interest rates of major banking institutions, like: the Federal Reserve, the European Central Bank, the Bank of England and the Bank of Japan must be considered. This shows the importance of the global trends.

To make a better move, the defaults of the policies must be considered and the legal implications must be studied to prevent any sort of distorted decision on the bases of these sources of information. However, this process will be slow but worthwhile as having a clear view of newer markets will make the process easy especially when interest rates are unstable or when market is expected to be subject to constant fluctuations and when some regions are overloaded with supply.

. . .

UNDERSTAND PAST:

After attaining the knowledge of particular currency pairs along with the definite idea of the current information about the international economy, history must not be ignored as it is famous for repeating itself and the past must be analyzed deeply to prepare for unforeseen situations. Looking at the past will help to recognize the present strengths and opportunities of each currency; also, it will help to predict the expected time of the continuation of a phase.

To exploit this information fully for the best results, people will be desperate to trade when one economy enters post-bust phase and the other one is in this stage already. In such conditions, the finance sector will be more helpful and benefit could be gained from the risks as compared to any other condition of industry.

BE AWARE OF VOLATILITY:

To know whether the investment is favorable or not, the current level of stability must be considered. As compared to other methods, this one is easier because it just involves focusing on stock markets of the associated economies.

The stability of future markets is the reason behind it. Stock market is most stable when the expected risks are lowest as lower expected risks help to penetrate into new markets.

The peak of boom is the most favorable time to increase levels of risks as this is the time when the interest rates, default rates and instability are at their the lowest while the bust phase is the one where the instability is higher with higher interest and default rates thus, it will be an unfavorable time to increase risks.

DECIDE ON BEST CURRENCY PAIRS:

The last thing to do is to identify the right currency pairs to trade after having a clear picture of the market for instance, where it is and for how long will it stay at that phase. For determining currency pair, the gap between the interest rates of two currencies must be determined. It must be understood that where each pair stands and how close to each other are they expected to stay as well as with proper distribution.

The conclusion can be reached by considering two variables, namely: related unemployment measurements and variance in the output gap. The gap and unemployment rate is inversely proportional as when the gap rises, more people get employment and the lack of man resource will result in inflation thereby increasing interest rates unless the economy is stable. The chart can explicitly explain the variation in the interest rate due to changes in the discussed variables.

Moreover, the balance of payment is the key indicator in determining the strength of the currency of any concerned nation. This is understood by comprehending the debt to capital ratio since the favorable the ratio, the stronger is the currency at unfavorable times. Calculation of this ratio requires you to understand the current account, capital and immediate position of each nation. This will assist you to conclude the underlying factor of the nation's immediate position, which can be assets, sales or cash at bank or capital invested in foreign or accumulated reserves.

Economic Indicators to Watch

There are only a few significant economic indicators; however, to remain in competition in the future market, you need to be vigilant for numerous indicators in addition to the significant ones. Implementing on the said is very difficult as there is a gigantic assortment of economic reviews and other pertinent indicators that can be analyzed to foresee various sorts of patterns prior to their occurrence. The complete list is enormous and cannot be practically included but the choices mentioned subsequently will kick you off to head to success.

Beige Book:

Beige book is also officially called the Summary of Commentary on Current Economic Conditions and is published by Federal Reserve District. It not provides the reader with access to raw information but is user-friendly as it makes the reader understand different territorial affairs of the different members of the United States Federal banking districts. Traders can benefit from this to foresee the movement in the currency in the future as they can comprehend how the Fed deals with the matters in different events. Federal Open Market Committee Meeting is held 8 times each year and this book is issued before each meeting.

The beige book doesn't create much fuss as it does not provide anything new yet it aids in deciding the right path to determine the movement of currency in the future. For instance, if the beige book stresses indicators that will raise inflation then you can be guided accordingly to make essential updates in plan concerning expected decline in the USD interest rate.

Consumer Price Index:

A consumer price index is a scale to determine a nation's economy and present state of inflation. It analyzes a consistent base of items that remain steady over the years, using a basket method. These items include toiletries and various other general groceries, along with day to day services including the cost of hair cut or an oil change.

These figures can be stratified into various strata like Workers and Customers, Workers include urban wage earners and Clerical workers, and customers refer to urban customers. The consumer price index for the available data of urban customers needs to be analyzed in detail as it changes drastically over the year. In the US, the present percentage appears in contrast with the year 1982 so changes must be resolved depending on record levels. Figures are then expressed in a run rate of development to allow brokers to anticipate results from the expected inflation.

Then, the chain-weighted consumer price index observes a significant shift with regards to the relevancy. This index gives a numerical representation of client buying arrangements when contrasted with different indexes. For instance, Customers jump from one brand to another due to price change, this behavior can be determined by only the chain-weighted index

Notwithstanding significant economic indicators like these, the consumer price index is taken as the final reference to determine the latest economic status of the nation. It is published monthly, which can be a definite source to understand movement for any related currency sets.

DURABLE GOODS REPORT:

This is a monthly report which includes all important updates about the measure of durable products manufactured in a country. A durable product is referred to products with an average life expectancy of more than 3 years; these products are capital in nature. Roughly 100 various industries that fall under this current report's domain are associated with the manufacturing of such products as cars, semiconductors and wind turbines. The numbers for a given nation will be given in the cash of that organization alongside a level of progress for the month over month numbers. A quarter of a year of modifications is additionally made part of each report. Information from this report is one of the 10 center segments of the US Conference Board Leading Index which is utilized to divine future development in the worldwide market.

While reading these reports , we must be aware of the fact that these numbers are exclusive of the transportation merchandise or things made by the defense segment as they will be unpredictable enough to slant things significantly one way or the other. Consequently, on the off chance that you need the full story in a given nation, you should do your due perseverance and track these numbers down for yourself.

As a rule, the durable products report is very convenient and handy for smart dealers to get a reasonable review of business demand in explicit nations. This is the situation because these sorts of durable products will, in general, require a greater investment which, consequently, shows that entrepreneurs and buyers are both acting with more prominent certainty, without their confidence being shaken away by unfavorable economy.

In light of the discovered outcomes, you may likewise discover it equally important to analyze subjects like the variation that happens with regards to stock and shipment ratios over a lengthy timeframe besides the growth rate of shipments and related stocks. When seen collectively, these ought to give a complete understanding of whether the supply is surpassing demand or the other way around. As durable products require lengthier manufacturing period than transient merchandise, the durable goods report can prove to be an exceptional method to get an early understanding of the forecasted profit increments for the upcoming month as a convergence of orders in a single month is a positive sign that more earnings are expected in future.

EMPLOYMENT COST INDEX:

The employment cost index is a very crucial economic factor that is made public every quarter every year. It stresses workforce cost to organizations established within the nation on, individual basis, average basis and analytical change in the costs with comparison to the last quarter. This report includes all perquisites and allowances related to workforce namely, employee benefits, hourly wages, bonuses and any related premiums for different industries other than state-owned agencies and farm workers as these would slant the numbers at either end of the range.

The gathered information is then categorized under different industries before being further disintegrated, to know that all the related data has been grouped. The further disintegration of the gathered information will make it easy for the dealers to identify early signs of expected inflation. Employee cost is the significant portion of the total costs borne by an organization and it is presented against the revenue generated from specified goods and services being offered.

In light of the general viewpoint, it can be said that the entire course of any currency is set by the employee cost index as when its report show drastically different results from those provided by other estimates, this single report will change the direction of the currency. The reason behind this relation is that these costs are to be ultimately borne by the customers which will have an unfavorable effect on the GDP projections if not corrected in the long run. This is also one of the crucial factors in deciding a nation's expected rate of productivity. The pace of variation in productivity and compensation costs shall go together as if the rate of compensation costs exceeds the rate of productivity, then the currency will progress towards devaluation.

Focus on Interest Rates:

Next to the complete understanding of the market and particularly significant currencies come the factors on which the brokers rely on for deciding transactions in the future market. This factor is the distinction in interest rate for different currencies. This is an essential process to shape an exact judgment on the qualities of different significant national banks, which consequently gives a clear picture of the general circumstances.

To completely understand the concept you are required to analyze unemployment measurements of nations under observation along with the loopholes in outcomes that each has. If an inverse relation is identified between the economy and workforce, inflation will rise and thereby increasing rates overall. Eventually, state banks will impose higher interest rates unless the economy hits the path of stabilization, focusing on these patterns will give you a complete understanding of what your subjective examination has uncovered.

Observing **Every Nation's External Position:**

To get a complete picture of currency or currency pair, it is crucial to observe how healthy are the present balance of payments. If there are two nations under analysis; first with asset sales and cash at the bank which can dissolve or redirect frequently, and the second with long term commitments for example accumulated reserves and foreign direct investment, then the first one will be less sustainable.

9

TECHNICAL ANALYSIS

Technical analysis is a process, or a tool utilized to forecast the estimated future price movement of a specified asset or security, like a currency pair or inventory. Technical analysis is based on market information. Technical researchers stress their understanding that past price trend and transactions of security plays a vital role in forecasting the future price variations of the security. One way is to utilize technical research together with the idea of base value indicators while the other method involves the application of technical analysis on other research commitments, yet the analysis depends exclusively on a security's factual outlines. Technical analysis and fundamental analysis are two primary techniques used to analyze securities and investment outcomes.

Technical analysis focuses on the contemplating patterns rather than breaking down the auxiliary attributes of security to understand the market sensitivity to variation in prices. The fundamental analysis stresses an in-depth examination of the financial statements of the organization to assess the value of the business. Two noteworthy presumptions structure the system of the procedure of technical analysis:

- Markets perform well with values that indicate factors that influence the cost of a security
- Price movements follow a regular pattern which can be observed through previous trends as they are typically rehashed ceaselessly after some time
- The efficient market hypothesis (EMH) implies that a security's market cost at a particular time implicit all accessible data and represents the security's real value.

This supposition is backed up by the conviction that the cumulative information of all the members in the market is denoted by the security's prevailing market price. This conviction is easily affected by external factors like declarations and news about security which can bring long term or transient effects on the cost of security. Technical analysis possibly works if markets are feebly proficient. As of late, three principle suppositions set up technical analysis:

- **Market Discounts Everything:**

TECHNICAL ANALYSIS just considers value developments, disregarding each essential variable of the market; hence it is disliked by numerous budgetary specialists. As per technical analysts, the value of the stock comprises of all from the basics of an organization to market psychology to expansive market variables, thereby, no need remains to look into other variables independently before settling on an investment choice. The only thing considered by the technical analysts is the value development; the changes in the value over some time are taken as a result of demand and supply of the specific stock in the market.

- **The Nature of History is Repetitive:**

The technical analysts emphasize that the pattern of value development followed in the past is an iterative process since, value development is generally based on market psychology which is dependent on feelings like fervor or dread, and these feelings can be predicted easily. Thereby, technical analysts use graphs to examine successive market development and feelings to comprehend market patterns. Even though major types of technical analysis have been available for as far back as century, they are as yet thought to be pertinent and helpful because they clarify trends in value development that is iterative in nature.

- **Movement of Prices is in Trends:**

TECHNICAL ANALYSIS CATEGORIZES the progression of value in long-term, short-term and medium patterns. Consequently, the core belief of numerous technical analysis methodologies is based on the presumption that the value of a stock will probably be as per the past patterns rather than moving arbitrarily.

Value of trading instruments like currency pairs, bonds, stocks, and futures are anticipated by technical analysis as they are affected by the intertwining relation of demand and supply. Many consider technical analysis as the assessment of the influence of demand and supply as reflected in securities market value developments. Generally, the technical analysis considers advancement in value, yet, other factors like open interest rates and trading capacity are also analyzed by few analysts. To aid with technical analysis trading, specialists have formulated numerous signs and trends over the business, along with various types of trading frameworks to help them in anticipating and trading on the advancement of values. A few pointers are intrigued basically in finding the most recent market pattern; these indicators are identified as resistance and support areas. Some indicators are also associated with the quality of a pattern and the likelihood of its coherence. Momentum indicators, channels, moving averages, and trend lines are some of the most commonly used technical indicators and charting methods. For the most part, technical analysts observe the following indicators:

- Chart designs
- Oscillators
- Moving Averages
- Resistance and support levels
- Price patterns
- Momentum and volume signs

Among many other philosophies or investment strategies, technical analysis and fundamental analysis are both poles apart. Numerous people apply both approaches in assessing and anticipating subsequent patterns in the prices of securities.

The fundamental analysis assesses security using its base value. Fundamental analysts consider all external aspects from the budgetary status and board of firms to general business and financial conditions. Thereby, all the components of the financial statements including assets, liabilities, revenue, and cost are integral highlights to the fundamental analysts.

Technical analysis is entirely different from fundamental analysis as the only integral highlights in focus are value and quantum of the securities, because they believe all other basic factors are incorporated in the value itself, consequently, there is no compelling reason to isolate them. Technical analysis does not take into account the base value of the security rather it examines graphs to consider and distinguish patterns and trends that can help anticipate the subsequent action of stocks. The economic rule of the efficient market hypothesis (EMH) is the biggest hindrance to the skill of technical analysis. Accordingly, this theory states that all the past and present data depicts the behavior of market prices, and there is no way to profit by mispricing and trends to produce extra benefits or alpha.

From the viewpoint of economists and analysts having firm faith in efficient markets, history does not repeat itself and historical price and volume data is not there for the information acted upon by people. On the contrary, they believe in the undefined fluctuations in price. It is also said that technical analysis does not provide a self-fulfilling prediction, which is the reason why it can have good performance in some areas.

An example of this can be that the majority of experienced traders have their stop loss less than a company's moving average of 200 days. Then, the stock might get forced down if there are a lot of sell orders resulting from the stock meeting this price by a lot of traders making this move.

What this does is ascertains the expected outcome. Afterward, the trend will remain strong as other traders will be selling their positions so that the price doesn't get decreased. Although there will be an initial temptation of selling, the asset will become so much more expensive after some weeks or months. The movement predictions of the signs will begin to come to life once a number of people have used similar signals. With that being said, traders would lose their control over the price with the passage of time.

Understanding Charts and Their Time Frame

How much time is needed for determining the trend and for the direction to take shape? When should you start acting on it? Is it necessary to take the action only after waiting for minutes, hours, or days? Price charts are analyzed for the prediction of price movements for technical traders and it's all due to the cyclic movement of normal market. The considered time frames and certain technical indicators of the trader are the key primary variables for technical analysis. It is possible for the technical analysis time frames that are shown on charts to follow yearly, monthly, or minute time formats. 5-min chart, 15-min char, 4-hour chart, hourly chart, and daily chart are the time frames that catch most of the attention from technical analysts.

- Daily chart
- Hourly chart
- 4-hour chart
- 15-minute chart
- 5-minute chart

A trader's time frame can be normally determined by the fashion of their trading. Weekly, hourly, and 4-hour charts are the most popular for analyzing markets when it comes to day traders who have only a day for opening and closing trading positions. Day traders are often looking for conditions that can cause price fluctuations in one trading day which yields profits and thus, consider 15-minute price movements to have high significance. However, there are no long-term trading uses or particular significance of this information in terms of charts dealing with days or weeks.

Candlesticks

Traders often construct charts of price movement indications with the use of the charting technique known as candlestick. A candlestick can be constructed from the price action in a single instant regardless of the time frames. The price action per hour can be noted by candlesticks based on an hourly chart, and the price action for every 4 hours is indicated by those based on 4-hour chart. When it comes to candlesticks, the highest and lowest price for the period is presented by the highest and lowest points of the candlestick.

The opening and closing prices for the period are indicated by the candlestick's "torso" and "body". The closing price (candlestick's top) is said to have exceeded the opening price (candlestick's bottom) if the body of there's a blue candlestick body in the chart. Also, the opening price is said to have exceeded the closing price for a red candlestick body. It is up to you to decide the candlestick colors, but black and white are mostly preferred by traders. However, you can opt for other color combination as well, such as yellow and blue, and green and red.

Regardless of your selected colors, it becomes possible to see the closing of prices is lower or higher at a period. The analysts can access other hints and patterns through candlestick charts, which is why they're preferred over regular bar charts.

Possible market reversals and trend changes are mostly estimated through the indicators that include candlestick patterns based on one candlestick or two to three candlesticks at once. Examples of this include the Doji candlestick that shows the market indecision that could indicate trend change or a hindered market reversal. There are no changes in the height of the candlesticks, which is a straight line accordingly. This can be attributed to its main characteristic which is the similarity in the opening and closing prices. The low-to-high range at the time frames is represented by the Doji candlestick's upper and lower "tails" or "shadows", which, if long, show the enforcement in the chances of market indecision or possible reversal. The Doji candlesticks come in different types. The standard type is called long-legged Doji where there is spreading of prices in directions, opening and closing in the price range mid for the time frame. The market indecision is distinctively indicated by the candlestick's form. A trend change in a different direction or hindered market indecision is mostly indicated when there's the formation of a long-legged Doji or other such Doji once the market has experienced extended uptrend or downtrend. Buyers get all the bad news from the gravestone Doji, which works as the opposite of the Dragonfly Doji.

The gravestone Doji can be used to indicate a hindered downside reversal since it represents that a purposeful attempt of increasing market prices was forcefully rejected. The probability of a forthcoming upward reversal can be seen by drawing the Dragonfly Doji once there's an extended downtrend. It is possible to logically interpret its formation by seeing how it depicts the price action analysis. The market indecision is indicated by the uniquely-structured four-price Doji, which is drawn when there is closing of the market in the middle of conducts and opening of buying and selling at similar prices at the same periods. This Doji is for markets that can move in all directions.

There is availability of a lot of different pattern types and candlestick formations. There is great significance of understanding the indications of candlestick patterns. However, it is also important to make sure whether there have been enough tests on their preciseness and accuracy. Traders are more likely to make more profits by rightly performing technical analyses. With that being said, one shouldn't just to stick to thinking about what they're going to do with all the money they make and actually spend a lot of time and make efforts to analyze how to have better management and risk limitation in case of wrong market predictions.

COMMON TECHNICAL ANALYSIS Mistakes and How They Can Be Avoided

When you employ a technical indicator, you actually place a barrier between yourself and the analysis as many traders depend a lot on technical indicators and they fail to acknowledge that these signs come from price.

Following are the mistakes that a trader makes when he uses a technical analysis and there are ways to prevent them:

Less Visual Attention:

For movements of price, the most acknowledged indicator is eyes. There is no barrier between the eyes and price. All the indicators and strategies in your chart only distract the focus of eyes and interfere with the visual price sensing. While making your decisions, this form of arguments can save you from making mistakes. This is good for a beginner trader. It is encouraged to begin with basic and simple analysis of visuals.

Forgetting Time-Frame Analysis:

Weekly timeframe analysis is usually forgotten by the traders when they use the technical analysis, chart analysis and patterns. They consider the daily frame analysis. You will be surprised to read the number and clues that you will get from the daily and weekly charts. Time is important factor that you use when you make your analysis. With short time frame, the analysis of chart is less clear, while the weekly charts gives better and fundamental results, and actual resistance and support lines gives authentic meanings, as they work for a longer time.

The professional traders usually start with the analysis of weekly charts and analyze the primary trends and its strengths. Next, they study about the daily charts and makes sure that the flair is going in the forecasted manner. While studying the daily charts, the traders set the entry and exit points to be used during the trading process. If you follow this procedure, it can put some drastic effects on the analysis when you shift to daily time frame. It is advised to make use of your eyes more instead of employing more ambiguous and complex technical indicators. You can properly make use of technical indicators, if you have understood the charts. New charts are preferred in the beginning. It is a fact that most of the top traders around the globe rely more on the eyes in comparison to the technical indicators. Make sure that your analysis includes different time frames; do not think that you do not need daily and weekly charts, or that they are of less use, if you are a day trader. The stocks tend to adhere to indexes about 70% of the time: this clue is associated with the indexes and broad market.

You must consider yourself as a technical trader if you are a day trader. For decision making, you must consider the price action and charts. Only volume shall not be considered. You shall be able to better understand how to play with volume in trading.

Learning Several Approaches to Technical Analysis

The classification of technical analysis is done based on the different perspectives of the technical analysts. The charts are approached by analysts differently and data is gathered about the behavior of prices. Following below are some of the different approaches employed by technical analysts:

Dow Theory:

This theory is proposed by Dow. The indexes in market and theory involved promoted the sale of newspapers; they also helped people to make money through trading. The traditional technical analysis is based on the Dow Theory. Dow contributed that securities flow in a pattern and these trends make patterns which can be identified by the traders, and unless a big change occurs, these trends remain unchanged. The entire market performance is forecasted by the Dow Jones Transportation Average and the Dow Jones Industrial Average. The Dow Jones Industrial Average is not a prominent indicator in the modern market as per the belief of most technical analysts, but the Dow Theory is still used for research and analysis.

Candlestick Charting:

This chart is designed by the traders in the Japan, and dates long back in the history. The direction of prices in the coming years is deployed by using different colors and shapes in the candlestick. These are used by traders for analysis.

Elliot Wave and Fibonacci Numbers:

You can also call the Fibonacci series as the Fibonacci numbers or Fibs. This is a series of numbers that is calculated by adding up the 2 preceding numbers in the series that begins with the 2 initial numbers on the number line: 0,1,1,2,3,5,8,13,21,34. That is 0+1 =1, 1 +1 = 2, 1 + 2 = 3, 3 + 5 = 8, and the same continues until infinity. So when the series exceeds to a double-figure, the ratio of a certain number to the subsequent one is 0.618. Golden ratio is the term given to this ratio. This value shows that dividing the larger number (out of the two) with the sum of 2 numbers is equal to the number obtained by dividing the smaller number with the larger number. Ralph Elliot is the man who designed the Elliot wave. He believed that the market moves in waves in the longer term which is shown by the Fibonacci series. According to Elliot, a bull market includes 5 up waves and 3 down waves. It is further added that that levels of resistance and support are located below highs and above lows at 61.8 per cent. If a security drops 61.8%

below a high, it is the right time to buy. Investors and traders use the system to pinpoint market trend that was appropriate for their time frames. Financial experts argue that it is highly incontestable that the action of a trader in the stock market would conform to the same order as the ratio of the spiral.

Gann System:

There are lot of mysteries and mythologies in the Gann system. It was adopted by some traders while it was also rejected by most of the traders. Gann created this system on the basis of astrology. In the recent times, the Gann system is dependent on "the relation between time and price". When a security shifts by a single point in a single day, it indicates 1*1 Gann angle which is considered to be a normal trade. When a security in single day shifts by two points, the trend is said to be bullish and creates 2*1 Gann angle. On the other hand, the bearish trend is reflected by an angle less than 1*1. To and fro movement of the market was observed by Gann in case of upward or downward trend. Gann system considers the fluctuation of price over time besides dealing with orderly retracements.

10

BITCOIN, ETHEREUM AND OTHER CRYPTO-CURRENCIES

The query whether crypto-currencies follow structured chart behaviors similar to the normal economic markets has been presented by several traders. Admittedly, crypto-currencies similar to Bitcoin and Ethereum act very well owing to the dearth of elementary players whose supposition can be opposite to the actual behavior of crypto-currency prices. These charts are unpredictable when it comes to fluctuation of price but can be effective as far as the prediction of the potential behavior of price is concerned.

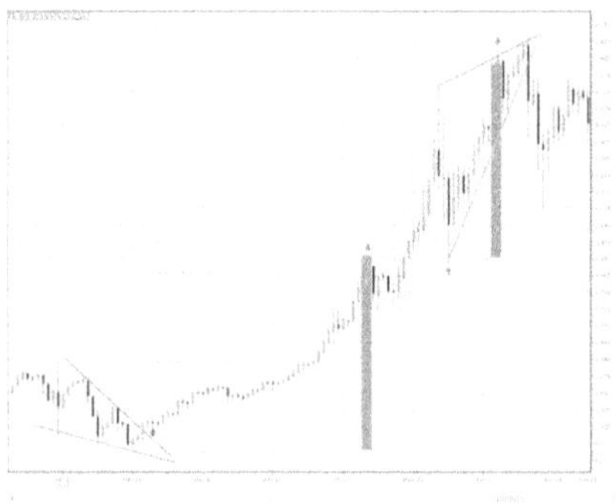

The above mentioned is the bitcoin day to day graphical representation.

The effective representation of basic graphical patterns across this period is evident from left to right side of the graph.

The upper points on the graph show the breakout of a falling wedge to determine the initial point of the wedge.

The breakout of the consolidation zone is directed upwards. The target is labeled thus stopping the move.

The upper target estimated by the block keeps the trend moving upwards leading to fulfillment and beginning of a stronger pullback.

The breakout of the rising wedge is directed towards the downside. The results are indicated in the next chart.

The breakout of the rising wedge is followed by the pullback from an extended move.

A measured move target that is ready is likely to bring about the multi down leg.

The measured move target can also be achieved by the tagged wedge break target. This eliminates the need to go low.

As the falling wedge is considered unusual pattern of topping, there was an expectation of year-high test.

The step by step explanation is given to facilitate your understanding.

The fundamental graphical pattern will represent the reasonable forecasting power on near-term price movements, as long as a standardized market exists for the trading of any instrument. In other words, if the trader is only focused on his profits, the graph pattern will depict the expected outcomes of market behavior. Since different types of people are engaged in crypto-currency trade and financial markets, it's obvious that the fluctuation of price will also be different for both types of trades.

Due to the introduction of futures contracts on Bitcoin, however this situation is changing. This enables the experienced trade firm employees to trade crypto-currencies under the protective regulations offered by various exchanges such as Chicago Board of Trade and the Chicago Mercantile Exchange. It is expected that the huge financial organizations will shortly take over the current crypto-currency players.

To sum it up, Bitcoin is expected to act similar to a developing regulated derivatives market. Due to the possible use of arbitrage algorithms for trading Bitcoin with financial institutes, greater correspondence is seen between the price actions of the bitcoin and other financial markets. Contrary to the claims of bitcoin promoters, bitcoin is now becoming the financial tool intended to serve a particular purpose.

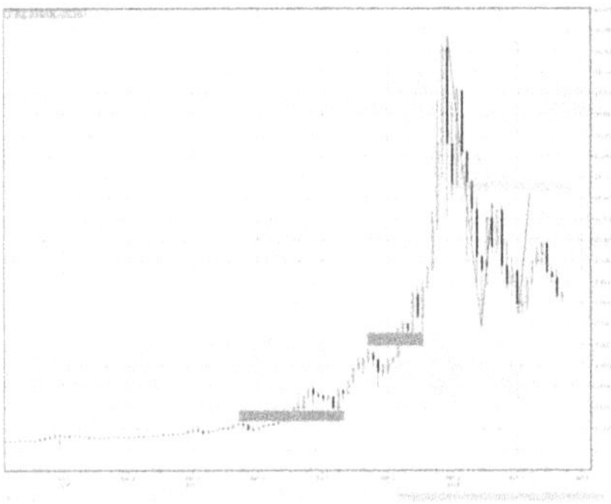

The next move of the bitcoin is still the main query forwarded by many after it deviated from the ever-high of 19666. It must amaze many that the stock market bottom with S&P 500 is printing a low of 666. The main thing here is not if there is any conspiracy involved behind this and we will only focus on the facts depicted from charts.

The chart shown above shows the Bitcoin details.

In year 2017, a couple of pockets were left behind by the massive upwards movement towards the blow-off. It was expected that the higher one will be tagged; however, it did not occur till now. This implies that Bitcoin is still expected to trade between

5500 and 5600 prior to trading over 12600 which was its level at 2017 closing.

The movement of the bitcoin to the 2017 closure of 12600 from the existing level of trading over 7000 (May 2018) will be considered as the complex multiple leg move. This movement is expected to be followed with immediate selling most probably targeting the low pockets.

Considering the time taken by the bitcoin to move above 19000, it is logical to expect the bitcoin to require similar time period to grasp this move.

It is appropriate to check the bottoming of the bitcoin as long as there is no formation of weekly level bottom pattern. Although it may require a lot of patience by Perma bulls to wait for the bottoming of bitcoin, it is worth waiting since it may fell down boundlessly.

Ethereum

The peak of the bitcoin was followed by the peak of various other crypto-currencies particularly Ethereum which showed a rise to maximum position in January 2018. This may be attributed to the hype created by Bitcoin at that time. More interesting is the fact that Ethereum doubled even after the fall of bitcoin. Such a movement was new for the Ethereum however; bitcoin has seen this up and down many times.

Three downside pushes are evident from the Ethereum's pullback structure. The Ethereum put an end to this move prior to reaching the third downside target. This was done through the resistance trend line's breakout shown by an upward arrow.

The breakout lead to an upwards move towards the peak of the channel due to the swing lows developed in the pullback process.

It resulted in a situation where second swing held more importance. Currently, Ethereum is being traded at this zone (as at end of May 2018). In case of maintenance of this level, we can expect an upward move towards the start of the pullback as per the indication of the three pushes down pattern. The highest-ever level of Ethereum is the start of pullback. The potential situation of the bitcoin is different from this situation of Ethereum.

However, this is not that simple. The daily charts still reveal a downtrend with a strong resistance being shown by the down channel top. Ethereum will not move upwards and will be kept low as long as the channel top is not cleared. The channel top will cause the Ethereum to break the record of the lowest level made in May 2018. Keeping the channel midpoint as the main target, even lower prices are expected. Currently (as of end of May 2018), the mid-channel level is almost 300.

Crypto-Currency is Not Money

In my opinion I must clarify the fact that crypto-currencies would not be able to rule the world in their current position as claimed by their promoters. They are not a valuable source or a monetary form. Although the concept of the significance of the crypto-currency for restoring trust was reasonable, it could not yield the desired results because of technological issues and issues in practical execution. However, no significant harm was caused to the assets.

The longing to make money from technological advancements

led to the emergence of various ideas. In particular, the advent of crypto-currencies is expected to bring revolutions in the future transactions. This is quite different from the dot.com scenario wherein some of the participants managed to survive. It is expected that the crypto-currency concept will bring about technological advancements causing massive revolutions in all aspects.

It is not easy to determine the crypto-currency that can endure the current bearish market trends. Even if one determines the right kind of crypto-currency, it is expected to lose its significance with the technological advancements in the similar manner in which the advent of Facebook rendered the previous social media platforms as obsolete.

Trading in crypto-currencies must involve a lot of caution on part of the trader since it is a hazardous play. It is better to understand the risky nature of crypto-currencies so that you don't put the amount you cannot afford to lose for betting. This statement is right for all types of trades. There is no emphasis on the management of risk to be the only factor of concern for the survival of a trader in this market.

11

MANAGING YOUR MONEY

The value of money management for being a good trader cannot be emphasized sufficiently. Speaking of a person's day trading process, a person has to have a very stringent method of money management. It should initially be decided how much you will risk and keep to this amount in your day-to-day trading efforts.

Day trading is already competitive and every day, computer-operated algorithmic trades are making it even more complex. Many traders invest bigger in their day trading account or involve in short-term trading or even gambling and tend to lose more money. Awareness about market terms like tender price, ask for price and exit and entry price is extremely important for making the most of money management. You will exchange more profitably as you gain more experience and expertise.

The long-lived advice of "plan your trade, and trade your plan" is another important and essential step in becoming a successful trader. Since these reduce the chances of losing money, the odds of your profits are maximized in every exchange.

To gain optimum profits through trading, always plan first

since it is already known that; if you fail to plan, you plan to fail. You will end up making a loss if you lose confidence in your skills and your trading strategy, and particularly if you hold a position in the market. You have to manage trading so as to make profit at the end of the day despite all the losses faced. You need to grasp how trading strategies operate during the day.

A successful trader has to put in money and time despite all the best instruments and trade strategies. Many traders mistakenly think they can generate money without investing in a huge effort by following some wonderful strategy. They need to understand that behaving with rapacity; panic and selfishness contribute to a stock market collapse. It is better to learn which trading strategy and techniques of market money management work best with your type of trading.

IMPORTANT MONEY MANAGEMENT **Rules for Traders:**

As a trader, you also manage your financial burden and decide with respect to your risk tolerance scale. To protect your investments, to maximize profits and to reduce your losses, the following rules for managing your money may be pursued:

PRACTICE TRADE SIZING:

Do not invest more than 10% of your stock trading capital in a single trade, for example, if you have a capital of $25,000, you may not use more than $2500 in any one of your trades.

KEEP STRICT STOP LOSSES:

It is recommended to set the minimum mental stop loss of 10 percent and a hard stop loss of at least 20 percent on inventories worth more than $10. A mental stop loss means that the loss you make with respect to a particular stock cannot exceed 10%. Assume that you evaluate your portfolio at the end of the day and note that one stock is showing a loss greater than 10%. You must then look at the product closely, and review the reports about the related company to see what caused this drop in the price of your products. On the other side, hard stop losses are legitimate stop orders placed by the traders. These often serve as a means of protection if there is an unpredicted shift in the market behavior.

Book Profits:

Partial profits are best attained at 40 percent or higher. It implies that you should sell part of the stock if it shows a rise of 40 percent or more and hold the part of the stock for later trading. You can recover the amount equal to or more than your initial investment in this way.

TRAILING PROFITS:

After making a profit of 15%, push your stop loss to the point of break-even and as long as you are in that position, try to achieve that; hence this is called trailing stop. You will consider using such a strategy following the initial benefit of 15 percent.

STAY AWAY FROM MARGIN TRADING:

It is significant to use margin trading sensitively to prevent suffering from the loss greater than your initial investment. Speaking of margins, they are usually a good way to grow your wealth in primary stocks. But on the other hand, such a stock investment technique may lead quickly to huge losses if not carefully observed and properly performed. The sayings of a recognized trader can be quoted to sum this up. He said that bigger issues arise when one assumes bigger positions.

. . .

SMALL AND STEADY WINS RACE:

Begin with little money and slowly but steadily grow your self-confidence and your business account. Don't aspire immediately to get wealthy. You could gradually increase your capital exposure if you have continuous trade returns following a long period (more than one year) particularly if you remained consistent even when market is facing hard times.

Diversify:

Let us assume that you have invested in 20 stocks following the rule of diversity and invested only 5% of your capital in each stock, and one of your options unexpectedly fails and you suffer a total loss with respect to that particular stock. This implies that just 5% of your market profits would have been wasted. You can survive and trade without serious harm. By contrast, if you do not have an effective money management strategy and there is less diversity in your transactions, bringing your entire capital to single trades will keep your profits going, and ultimately most of your trading capital can be lost. You might even be removed from the exchanges altogether.

CONTROL YOUR RISK:

It is advised to continue with a paper exchange practice program if you're new in trading. Keep your stock trading records in writing and track record all the feelings and errors you are experiencing during your business. After about a month, you are ready to trade with cash in reality. Do remember that major positions cause large problems.

. . .

Use Limit Orders to **Get in and Get out of Position:**

You may be provided with opportunities for trading in the market, however; the price may be different from your desired one. Most of the time, a limit order put close to the last closure is typically met since a stock normally retraces after the first part of the session.

Some traders cannot manage checking the stock throughout the day. The solution to this problem is the market order. Note that there may be fluctuation in the price you had to pay when your order is done

The biggest mistake investors make is to blindly follow a trade process. Despite the definite course of a process, several variables involved in the process must be considered.

Keep Eye on Brokerage:

Brokerage is the biggest eater of your investments although it is not taken seriously. Brokerage may involve concealed charges that may consume your profits and enhance your losses. The brokers sometimes behave selfishly and conceal the schemes that are profitable for you and offer the schemes bringing profits to them. This implies that it is important to check the brokerage schemes personally and not to blindly accept the schemes offered by broker. Moreover, the trading statement must also be checked.

12

TRADING PSYCHOLOGY

Now you need to be expert in another skill to ensure your grip on the market. This skill is technical skill of trading. The things mentioned till now explain this concept.

And the other skill required to master the market is psychological aspect of trade. The psychology of trade involves the mental capacity owned by a person to survive in this market. This is the most important feature of trade. It's also the most difficult skills to grasp. It may take you a few years to have a grip on it. The reason is that this skill is mostly learned through business trading which takes time also.

The sole purpose of this chapter is to direct you to the correct way so that you can enhance your learning over time and achieve the right mental framework.

Here I will give you some pro tips that you should always adhere to when trading, so you can develop the right mindset as the business demands.

Let's get started.

· · ·

Just like other things, trading is one of projects that only requires time and efforts; in start it seems very easy but this is not the first thing that most new entrepreneurs have in mind when they hear about it and get nervous regarding business.

To understand this in a better sense, I will explain it to you. We often found an advertisement while browsing through internet. Imagine you find an advertisement that says,

"Emerson makes $100 a day day-trading from his home. Find out how." This ad triggers you to think "What if I could make $100 daily? Then I may resign from my job." "Lots of people are earning from home. I may become one of them"

You respond to the advertisement. Now there is a business hack, the page has a video which triggers you to invest small amounts to make easy and quick money whenever it signals you.

After that you will find or listen many stories that how this work brought changes in their life. You will be convinced that mostly cases are of financially unstable people who became rich overnight working from that site.

Imagine you went to buy something, you start imagining bundles of money which you want to spend on picnic but have u imagined that after spending that on picnic how would you purchase new car, new house etc.

In short, after a month of using this system you get nothing after being promised. In real you had to pay $50000 and now you don't believe on internet's advertisements.

You should not be impressed by the quick and easy money-making. Trading can earn you money if you trade with patience and carefulness and put in time and effort.

Now think about the other aspects also. In case you don't know how many years it took to a student to become doctor, so here is the answer, it took 7 or more years to a normal person to emerge as doctor.

Trade is kind of tricky just like law, business; same as that a student pushes himself as hard as possible just to peruse his or her dreams. A businessman served his whole life to his business just to build his own business empire. Think about all the circumstances and conditions which a student and a businessman go through in his whole life. Then how could you expect that it took only few weeks and you will learn all the terms and condition of trade.

I simply mean that quick and easy money-making will lead you nowhere besides wasting your precious time and effort.

Trade is one of the most important ventures of the world. But to be successful in this field you must put more handwork, be more sophisticated more dedicated. But if you want to get success in this era you have to hard worker, and you need to be prepared to face both profits and loss in your venture. Ultimately, you will lead the trade scene.

Start Viewing **Losses as Part of Game**

In trading business, there is no place for the fancy world. And if you're thinking that such fantasy world does exist, then you must change your thinking. There is no surety in trading business; all we can do is to put our efforts, give our best and then wait for the results.

So basically, it's all about that how you manage the risk, and this is the only reason why risk management is one of the main subjects of the business studies. This explains how to make more money without the fear of losing and makes business easier.

It is statistically unmanageable to secure100% of the time. Losses are common in all types of business. A myth is generally prevailing that the Wall Street professionals possess higher wisdom than any of us which enables them to gain an inside edge. However, this is contrary to fact.

Jack D. Schwager is the author of "Market Wizards" (I personally liked it and it is a worth reading book). It reveals that a survey team interviewed the successful traders. They all concluded this fact that damages are the part and parcel of business and they admitted this point.

The worst times gives the best lessons to learn. It has been realized that the losses cannot be eradicated completely from business. With the passage of time, it is understood that managing the things in available resources is the only way to prevent losses. The same is struggled day by day. Hard work is the only key to success and you can attain it by practicing it in letter and spirit.

As a result, another idea struck my mind, in which, a proper approach needs to be implemented, where, if an individual is honest with his profession and he prefers his / her work on anything, then nothing can stop him / her from attaining success. Subsequently, this strategy may be corroborated with a practical demonstration to see the results. And, this idea will announce the sense of achievement or otherwise. With the practice, it would be realized that business is concluded with winners and losers and the key to successful business is to manage the losses effectively.

While doing this activity, you will build self-assurance in your practice. Going through a period of loss is one of the adverse challenges you will ultimately come across in this business (It is also referred to as a losing streak). This is basically the stage in which the system and the allied signals do not illustrate desirable performance.

If you do not have the abilities and knowledge to manage the losses in business, as it occasionally occurs, then you are likely to lose the contest. Nonetheless, if you have acquired the skills to handle the challenges during the course of business, then you can manage the situations. And in adverse circumstances, you would be aware that you need a pause and may resume after some time with good performance.

Hence, this fact must be realized from now onwards that losses in the business are inevitable. One would become less concerned, if the homework is already completed in all respects. You will have no trouble, if you follow the 2% rule of money management. With the acquisition of practical knowledge, you could take prudent decisions and can do the right things most of the time like other experts do.

Keep Trading as Part-Time Activity

If you take trading as a part-time activity, then it would help you ending up in a successful scheme in your professional life.

If you rely on trading as the sole source of income, then it would be very difficult to do the business successfully. Undoubtedly, such professional traders do exist, who earn with an aim to support families. However, a huge number of them are receiving a regular paycheck from their employer firms. And income from trading is treated as a bonus to monthly income. Same is the working mechanism of Wall Street.

The hedge fund managers as well as other money management professionals are considered as efficient traders since regardless of the level of their performance, the professional management fee is charged by these people.

If you may have a holistic view, money and profits made from the trading is not the only source of these professionals. This is possibly the reason of their expertise in the matter.

There is a clear-cut intention. The effective trading decisions are taken, when your overall objective is not the money only.

When there is a continuous pressure on you about the matters, like, "How would I give my child's school fees?" or "How rent of this month would be paid to the owner?" there are high chances that you will not be able to make efficient trading decisions. Subsequently, owing to the stress, you will tend to trade disproportionately or will do the un-necessary dealings in an impulsive attempt to make some income.

So, how that will be handled?

Find a day time job for yourself. Try to seek some work which you can always do part-time for financial upkeep and then the part-time trading could be carried out. As we already indicated, the swing trading strategies can be used, if you are employed at this time. A majority of people can handle this phenomenon and it takes a few minutes in a day to perform this analysis.

You can opt for trading when unemployed. Trading is open all day and night at certain markets like the Forex market which allows everybody to trade at some time of the day. People can take benefit of this flexibility.

You can learn so many things through freelance trading and by getting a day job. Primarily, you become stress free with respect to your financial affairs.

In addition, you gradually gain financial stability. The dream comes true, when you intend to invest and trade with an objective to become wealthy. The technique to invest and trade further is to save some money each month as it will help you grow financially.

Thirdly, the trading can and cannot result in stress. Handling the business affairs can be a difficult task. Moreover, you can immediately come across stress, especially if trading involves rapid loss and earning of money. There can be serious consequences, if you are merely thinking of using the money for your financial upkeep.

When your financial responsibilities are being taken care of in a well-organized way, then you can be in your comfort zone. With this, your mind works efficiently and generates constructive ideas. You will have to wait for right time to trade and get the opportunity to invest. In the course of these circumstances, your decisions on financial matters can increase your bank credit and can maximize your profits.

Cultivate Habit of Discipline

Discipline is extremely important for trading. Realizing the success in this business becomes very difficult, if you are not well-organized.

So what actually the discipline is? And what is the way to develop it?

The ability to follow the code of conduct or a definite set of rules is basically defined as a discipline. We can also say that it is the aptitude to practice and apply self-control besides preventing your permissive activities in a given condition.

A problem upsetting many traders who could not get consistent results in the markets is described as the lack of discipline. In fact, in most cases, the problem is not the lack of practical knowledge to carry out a task. It is the non-implementation of the theoretical knowledge

For example, during your exams, you have a clear-cut idea of doing study instead of enjoying outside, since the results will entirely depend upon your study and hard work. To be physically fit, you know the significance of exercise. Moreover, you certainly prefer to avoid the food stuff, which is not effective for your overall health. However, a few of the things are still wrongly done in one way or another.

Same scenario is observed in the event of trading. You have an idea to keep a stop-loss order besides strictly following it. However, in some way, you cannot remain consistent because you believe that the market will reciprocate all the times. Accordingly, your loss extends to the uncontrollable levels in due course.

Similarly, you also know that it is imperative to follow a right and proper trading system. Still, you keep pursuing the latest system.

It is evident to discover incorrect aspects. It is not enough to only know the scope of work. In-fact, a set of actions is required to maintain your discipline in a complete manner. Those actions comprise of:

PLAN EVERY TRADE **Ahead of Time**

Planning is important in every trade, since, if you fail to plan, then you are planning to fail.

It needs time to carefully analyze the situation besides formulating a set of rules to be followed. The given below points should be part of your plan:

1)_THE ANTICIPATED market setup

2)_The rules through which entry price is governed and controlled

3)_The rules to regulate and place your stop-loss order.

4)_The guidelines to place your take profit order.

YOU WILL BE okay and work will go smooth, if your plan contains the aforesaid aspects.

Ensure that you have noted them. Your plan should be well written and don't keep it limited to our mind. A plan must be brought in black and white. In any case, you also need to be determined to always adhere to your plan.

Revisit and consider your plan at the start of each day and prior to taking on any trade. With this, your discipline will be improved with the passage of time.

Keep Trading Journal

Another dynamic tool to possess is a trading journal.

Likewise, your life events on a certain day are recorded by a personal journal, the events happening on a typical trading day is recorded by a trading journal.

Regarding trading journal, every action which has taken place right before and after the commencement of the trade is recorded. Have you stood by the plan? Did you follow the 2% risk management rule? Did you anticipate the right set up prior to the action? Were you desirous of encouraging your stop-loss order or interested in hurriedly closing out the trade?

Everything should be recorded and maintained for its subsequent review.

The two key objectives are fulfilled by a trading journal. First of all, it keeps a record to review and analyze your actions at any given point of time; you can have a view of your right and wrong doings and have a better idea to prevent the repetition of the wrong action besides learning a lesson from it.

Furthermore, it maintains a complete registration track for your help and understanding. By considering it, you will put your best efforts to truly follow it and you will also try to prevent any mistake.

Hence, it is another tool, by which, your discipline can be developed in a desirable way.

Keep Physical Reminder

In this scenario, a simple note written by you is referred to as a physical reminder.

There are possibilities of making huge mistakes, when you make a little deviation from the original plan due to a certain reason. Damage may be in terms of cost and other factors. Almost, we all have come across such occasions in our past.

You might be involved in over-trading. Certain thing might would have occurred, like, premature arrangements, increase in your stop loss, and probably your practical merchandizing went opposite to that of original plan, due to which, a considerable financial loss was realized.

It should not be ignored as due to this ignorance, the chances of mistake are increased in future; simply write it down and paste it somewhere for your recollection. It can be pasted at your table or workstation or at any other prominent place for your observation.

This will remind you of your earlier mistakes and will caution you not to repeat the mistake and will keep you on a right and well-organized track.

To sum up, the trader and trading cannot effectively run without discipline. Your intelligence, acumen, knowledge and your previous performance and progress all are insignificant, if there is no discipline and self-restraint. Moreover, if you do not turn out to be a disciplined individual, then time will make you learn a lesson. With the help of above-mentioned tools, you will gain an insight of the phenomenon. In the series of our discussion, the last point of trading psychology needs to be explored now.

View Trading as a Game and not a way of Making Money

By and large, trading is actually a pleasing activity coupled with incentives and entertainment.

We are likely to overcomplicate it besides eliminating the fun part from it owing to certain reasons. It can be attributed to one of the causes of failure at trading. Redefining your view of the whole activity and start exploring it as a game can be one possible solution.

What is the first thing on your mind, when you imagine about a game?

Typically, games are linked with a lot of amusement. These are also considered as a way to emotionally and psychologically challenge ourselves. Besides, these are assumed to be the activities, wherein there are no real penalties in the event of losing the game.

The trading can also be seen in a similar way.

Imagine the trading as a game of points basically. The money you are investing is actually the points. Carefully playing the game besides collecting maximum points over time is the major objective of this game. It would be the natural phenomenon that at times, you are either winning the points or the other way around.

You can expand your activities with the accumulation of points. The accumulated points may also be used for practical use; however, it is not the point of concern. The main point is to demonstrate sportsman spirit. Never lose the courage and do what you love and love what you do. Passion and profession should be the same to attain success as hardships and challenges give you many lessons and inspiration to move further.

Observe your feelings and emotions? With your previous trading experience, you can better realize how it tends to remove almost all the stress? Can you notice the new avenues and growth opportunities for you? What would be the scenario, if you prefer to turn out to be a trader with these views and opportunities?

Let's have a comparison. Suppose, you are trading a $100, 000 business and in this month you gain 20% profit. Now, you are imagining "Hurray, I have got handsome amount and I could get a car!" Then, unpredictably, you witnessed a declining stage and hit a losing streak with a loss of 10%. Subsequently, you become sad and regretful, "The money, which has been lost, could also have been spent on a holiday." Or you mind advises you, "This money was equal to my two monthly salaries, Oh my God! How it all took place?"

Have you noticed the dissimilarity between these two aspects? One view is associated with enjoyment and fun and the other one makes you suffer from emotional ups and downs. Which one is the ideal and best way to be successful as a merchant?

If you are eager to get pleasure from this, you have to reshape the conventional money management skills. Then, you have to consider trading as a game of points to play and seek fun from it and not as a way of making money.

If you have the same point of view, you will be happy with the trading venture and your undertakings would go ahead smoothly as planned and as desired.

13

STEPS TO BECOME SUCCESSFUL TRADER

Although this information has thoroughly conveyed us so many remarkable trading strategies, which can be implemented to witness the success with respect to future trading, a combination of all or some of these strategies could allow you to easily use and implement them to really take the trading to new heights. Certain set of actions need to be taken at this point, for example, establishing the account and choosing the preferable strategy to be used in subsequent stages. However, there is a handy checklist in this chapter, which is available and accessible for your assistance in carrying out the practical trade. Now, we may explore that steps that are needed in executing a positive trade in buying and selling financial instruments.

Some Examples of Good Habits for a Stock Trader Really Useful for a Futures Trader

Building up Your Watch List

Conducting research and investigations is the first step to kick off the futures trading. Upon waking up at the start of day, have a view of your notes and your research summary. Subsequently, that information may be utilized to produce a good watch-list. This watch-list has a considerable significance since it allows you to focus on some selected choices only, which you can select for trading on that particular day. The market comprises of thousands of stocks. It would be very easy to pick the right stock for investment and you too can have this ease by creating this watch-list.

The watch-list can be created through various methods. However, use of a scanner is one of the ideal methods. With the help of these scanners, a specific condition is sought out of a stock and these can step up the things really faster even beyond your expectations. To achieve the target through the scanner, the requirements to be fulfilled need to be listed out. Afterwards, the scanner will alert you upon finding the desirable criterion.

This step has a few extensions. When the scanner displays a few stocks, then you need to carefully check them instead of just investing in the first ones on the display. When, the results are acknowledged on the scanner, you will immediately figure out the valuable stocks on which you preferably invest. On the other side, you will come across many of the stocks, which are no more required and you will overlook them simply.

Decide Which of These Stocks Work Best for You

When you have come across the stock related choices on the scanner, you can choose the best one out of these stocks. Also, you might have a particular plan in your mind to adopt and after a careful review; a stock is chosen that seems to be truly adhering to that plan. There is no daily restriction in changing the plans. You can also continue with one plan / strategy, if it is fulfilling your requirements.

As we already mentioned in some of our strategies, ensure that there is no trade from your side in the first five minutes of opening of the market. There are expert traders, who wait for more than these five minutes and even wait for longer, so that the stability in market patterns could be observed.

The market is relatively unstable at the start of the day and your profits can be ruined while investing at this time. Prior to investing in the stocks, if you carefully examine the choices on your scanner, you are about to penetrate into the market in just five minutes or so. Nonetheless, understanding this volatility besides preventing it is a really important aspect.

Put That Entry and Exit Strategy in Place

Since you now have some stocks that are ready, you must be excited about gaining entry into the market and beginning your trade. Prior to making the purchase, you have to determine your strategies. This not only refers to the overall strategy, but also the entrance and exit strategy so that you are aware of how to enter into and leave a market at the appropriate times.

You first need to determine your entry strategy. This signifies the place you are comfortable with and are going to buy your stocks from. You also seek to determine an entry point at a low cost so that you avoid spending too much of your money and make higher profits subsequently. When examining the graphs for that stock, you should be able to identify a safe entry point from where you will get an economical price for the stock.

Determining an exit strategy is also vital. You should have a point where you put a stop to your loss and to your profit. We will first discuss the stop for money loss. It often happens that the strategies you have selected or the decisions you have made do not end up according to your expectations, and you start losing money on that stock. This stop ensures that you are able to regulate the amount of money you will lose. When the stock attains this number, you are going to leave the market, irrespective of what happens to the stock afterwards.

In the absence of this stop, things might get too difficult for you. When several new traders observe the downfall of the stock, they continue trading with the hope that there will be a turn-around in the market. In some situations, the market does take a turn; however, there are also situations when market remains at a low position or keeps declining. If you do not have a stop, you may end up losing a large amount of money. In addition, if the market declines significantly, then it is likely that you are unable to meet your losses. Hence, it would only be logical to determine a stop, which is the point where you leave the market at a reasonable loss, before things get too difficult. You always have the option of entering the market at a subsequent stage when the market starts improving.

Once you have determined your stop loss, you should establish a profit stop. Many beginners may avoid this step as they presume that it would be best to just get through the market till they no longer make profits. However, it is determined by day trading that various highs and lows will be experienced by the market, even in quite stable markets. A profit stop is important since it would be a good idea to exit the market before the prices fall and you end up with no profits at all. It is likely that the market may become highly profitable and you are not able to make as many profits as you could have if you stayed in the market. However, there are also chances that the market falls and you end up losing your profits.

PURCHASE the Stocks You Want
Once you have developed your watchlist and established your

entry and exit strategies to remain on the safe side, you should actually enter into the market and commence your trade. You should determine all your criteria for the stock before you start trading. However, if you are following a particular approach that gives an overview of the criteria, you should simply stick to that.

If you are working with a broker when carrying out day trading, you will only have to give them the order to commence trading. A lot of information is going to be included in the order that allows the broker to work according to your requirements. It would consist of information on the kind of stocks you want to buy, the number of shares of each you want to buy, the money you are willing to spend, and when you want to enter and exit the market. The broker places your order in the system, taking into account this information.

You also have the option of carrying out the trade independently without a broker. Though this is also alright, many of the novice traders avoid doing so because they are concerned that they may make mistakes. If you do decide to do things yourself, make sure that you choose a good platform that enables you to carry out your trade swiftly. If the system is slow, or you make errors, you may end up messing up your trade.

Pay Attention to the Market Until the Trade Is Closed

You are going to realize soon that there are certain distinctions between day trading and other stock trading options. There are several other options that extend for the long-term; you buy the stock and then remain in the market with the hope that the selection you have made will rise up after a while. However, with day trading, the trade has to take place in a single day. The buying and selling of stock should all take place between the start and end of the same trading day.

Because of this, day trading becomes more risky in comparison to certain other stock trading alternatives. This suggests that you need to keep a watch on the market so that you can take rapid decisions regarding when to buy and sell your stocks.

Day trading benefits from the highs and lows that are experienced by the stocks during the day, and hence, it is quite unique. The charts of stocks show that in the long-run, their values remain quite stable. Certain news or other factors may be seen on the charts in the form of changes in the trend; however, on the whole, the stock value is more probably going to move up. However, when viewing a week or a day of past stock values, various minor highs and lows will be observed. These may not be very severe, but the fact is that they do occur. It is these highs and lows that day trading seeks to capitalize.

A day trader concentrates on keeping track of these ups and downs that take place during the day. This helps them in determining when to buy the stock and then determine when to sell them so as to attain the greatest profits, or to restrict the losses to as low as possible.

After you have started trading, you need to remain attentive to the market. Sometimes, rapid changes may occur in the market, which would require you to make rapid adjustments to your position, or close it so that you earn greater profits or incur minimum losses. In day trading, you cannot place your order and then take a backseat. Rather, you need to keep a close eye on the market. If you are unable to do so, then you should avoid placing an order.

Sell Your Stocks When They Reach Your Original Exit Points

The exit strategies discussed earlier are going to play a role at this point. These numbers are significant in day trading as they decrease certain risks associated with day trading and restrict the loss of money incurred when the market moves in a different direction than what you expected. Irrespective of the market condition, it is important for you to remain true to your entry and exit points. When you let your emotions control your decisions and disregard these points, you are going to face issues in achieving your goals.

You should adhere to your exit points at all times, i.e. when the market is declining and also when it is rising. It is easy for people to comprehend why they need to adhere to the exit strategy when the market is falling as they do not want to experience significant losses in the market. However, this is difficult for them to comprehend when the market is rising. They may have decided a stop regarding the amount of profit they desired to make, but when they see that the market is continuing to rise, they are reluctant to leave the market at that point.

Though it may be difficult to do so, you should ensure that you adhere to your exit strategy, even when the market is rising. It is possible that the market exceeds that point; however, it is also likely that it takes a sharp dip and you end up losing all the profit you had earned earlier. Hence, this is a way of making sure that your investment remains secure. If the market keeps on increasing, you still have the chance of entering it again later.

It would be a good idea to take out some time and review the trade, and later on, write a few of that information as research.

When starting off as a day trader, it is important for you to learn different things regarding the market. This becomes more important when you have not made any investments previously. A trader is supposed to learn along the way and make any changes that may be required. However, when you are getting to know about different strategies and the extensive number of trades that are carried out in day trading, it may become difficult to keep track of all the information.

You may experience the positive effects of obtaining a journal and writing down a few of your mistakes, tips and other aspects following each trade. It is not important for you to note down a large amount of information, unless you wish to do so. Writing some lines or a paragraph is sufficient. You may think that this is just a waste of time. However, if you ever purchase a stock after some time, or if you are trying to find out why you are stuck and unable to gain your desired profits, you may benefit a great deal from assessing this information.

14

HOW TO MANAGE YOUR RISKS?

To be successful at day trading, you mainly need to have three things. You should have a good psychology that is able to deal with the stress of this kind of trading, a group of trading strategies that will assist you in taking the right decisions and an appropriate plan to assist you in handling your risk. Your entire program will be unsuccessful if you are lacking in either of these things, and you may end up making no money in day trading.

Being a beginner, you may concentrate on just the trading strategy you have employed. Though the significance of the trading strategy cannot be denied, you cannot leave out the other two components that are also very important. If you have managed to come up with a suitable strategy to work with, it is not necessary that you have the self-discipline needed to remain true to that strategy or to patiently wait in the market. This is why you may not be gaining success, irrespective of the strategy you have chosen.

We will discuss risk management in this chapter. We can discuss the various strategies that may be adopted later as it is more important to first get to know about the rules that you should follow to handle your risk. It is quite likely that any strategy you select will sometimes result in an unsuccessful trade. The market does not always work the way it is expected to. However, when you learn how to appropriately manage your risk, you will be able to restrict your losses to a minimum.

While managing your risk, you first need to determine the exit point, which is the time when you will leave the market. For many people, pride may come in the way and it may be difficult for them to accept defeat or the fact that they did not judge the market correctly. However, if they keep on persisting with that trade, it is likely that they will end up losing a greater amount of money and make a more serious mistake that previously. Hence, it is important for you to learn when to decrease your losses and exit at the correct time.

Sometimes, the trade may not be in your favor. This is true for beginners, as well as for those who have been trading in the market for several years now. You should be ready to exit the market when the trade is no longer in your favor. Day trading often starts experiencing the unexpected because the market experiences high fluctuations from one point to another. One may find it difficult to accept defeat; however, you should remember that there are many other trades that you can become involved in at other times.

As a day trader, your main objective is to earn money. If you keep on persisting with a position that is against you only because you want to prove that you made the correct prediction, then you are actually not a good trader. You are supposed to make money, and not to show that you are never wrong.

To minimize your risk, you also need to adhere to the plans and rules inherent in the strategy you have selected. This is not that difficult when the trade is moving swiftly and you are making profits. However, when the trade is not going too well, you may want to go against the rules. You may feel that this is the right thing to do at that point; however, it may become quite costly for you. When you stick to the rules of the strategy you were following, you may lose some money. However, this amount may not be much and you may be able to enter the market again, which may not be possible if you incur a huge loss by not following the rules. A good idea is to accept few of the quick losses, exit the trade, and then enter again when things get better.

After this, you should ensure that you determine low-risk entries that can potentially offer you a high reward. These may still be a little risky, but their risk is considerably lower than you will experience with other stocks you select. The most ideal arrangement is one in which you discover an opportunity that offers you a trade with limited risk. For instance, taking a risk of $100 to earn $300 is a good arrangement; but if you are taking a risk of $100 to earn $10, then you have chosen a wrong trade. Majority of the professional traders will stay away from trades that do not offer a ratio of more than 2 is to 1 for profit-loss.

This suggests that if you buy a stock worth $1000 and are taking a risk of $100 on that stock, then you should sell that stock for at least $1200 to make it worthwhile and to reduce your risk. It is obvious that it may not always work out this way and you may experience a loss, for example when the stock decreases to $900. However, there should at least be a possibility that you can earn $1200. If it is only possible to earn $1100 on the stocks, there is very low profit-to-loss ratio and it would be better not to take the risk.

Sometimes, you are unable to determine a stock that has the correct profit-to-loss ratio, which is okay. It would be better to not be involved in the market for a day instead of trading on a stock that is not according to your requirements. You can start trading in a market after a while, in a few days' time, being aware that you did not end up losing your money in the process. The 2 is to 1 ratio puts you in a good position in the market. You may come across situations when you are not correct or the market does in an opposite direction as expected. However, if you remain true to this ratio or a better one, you have the leverage of being wrong for 40% of the time and still earn from day trading.

THREE QUESTIONS PERTINENT **to the Stocks and also to Futures Trader**

When you take the decision of buying a stock over a trading platform, you are putting some risk on your money. It is possible to face problems with even those stocks that are consistent with the ratio discussed earlier, and so you need to accept that some amount of risk is always present in your money in this process. Nonetheless, to manage this risk, you can take a few steps. You need to ask the following questions to yourself before carrying out any of the trades you have selected.

- Have I chosen the right stock or futures contract for trading? In risk management, the foremost step is to deal with the correct stock or futures contract. When you choose an unsuitable stock, you will end up facing loses no matter which instruments or platform you use. You should ensure that you are not becoming involved in stocks that are not moving at all, penny stocks that may be manipulated to a high extent, those with a small trading volume and those which are already being extensively traded by institutional traders and machines.

- How many shares or futures contracts should I buy? The next question is to determine the share size to work with. This is determined by the amount of money you have and your objectives for a single day. If you wish to achieve a target of just $1000 per day, then you will have to buy over 20 shares most of the time, or a single futures contract. When the amount of money you have in your account is not sufficient for this type of target, then you need to decrease your objective for a day.

- The final question is determining your stop loss. This is essentially the amount of loss you are willing to make in case the market goes in an opposing direction. You should never risk over 2% of the equity in your account. Hence, if there is $10,000 cash in your account, you should not put more than $200 at risk. This indicates that though your return on investment on your trades is not very high, you manage to save most of your money.

THREE-STEP RISK MANAGEMENT **Plan**

Step 1: The foremost step is identifying the absolute highest dollar risk that you would take for your potential trade. As a beginning, you are not recommended to risk over 2% of the equity in your account. However, depending on the amount of money you have and the degree to which you are ready to risk your money, you can increase or decrease this percentage. It is important that you compute this amount before commencing your day trading.

Step 2: the next step is to determine the highest risk per contract you will be taking, i.e. the stop loss for your strategy. This will be elaborated later on as your stop loss is dependent on the strategy you have selected.

Step 3: Calculate the highest number of contracts that can be used by obtaining the values from step 1 and 2. This will provide you with the highest number of contracts that you can trade at any time. Make sure you don't go over this level as it would make your risk too high.

To see how this works, consider an example. Suppose you have $40,000 in your account and you will buy a few futures contracts. When remaining true to the rule of restricting the risk to 2% of your total money, your risk would be limited to $800. We will adopt a conservative attitude for this trade as beginners and risk just 1% of the account, i.e. $400. This completes the first step.

Since you are keeping track of the futures contract, you take the decision of selling the short when it gets to $50, and you wish to get them covered at $48, with the stop loss fixed at $51. This suggests that you will be risking around $1 for each contract. It can hence be stated that the value of the futures contract is $400 for a move of $1. This is going to be step 2.

We will now move to step 3. The size will be computed by dividing the numbers in step 1 and 2 to determine the greatest size of our trade. In this example, we will be able to buy 1 contract at the maximum.

Making Sure You can Handle the Stress

A final point to be noted is that you should ensure that you are actually able to deal with the stress inherent in day trading. Day trading is a stressful activity. You cannot just purchase your stock in the market and then forget about them, checking only from time to time. Rather, you need to monitor the stocks the entire day. The small variations in the price of the stock throughout the day can influence your possible earnings, and this can make your day quite stressful.

If you do not have adequate time to give to this form of trading, at least on those days in which you decide to trade, then this investment option is not the correct one for you. If you are unable to handle the stress or are already experiencing a lot of stress in your life, then day trading is not appropriate for you. In addition, it is also not for your when you are not able to take good decisions at the last minute and are influenced by your emotions.

Day trading is an excellent investment option for you; however, you need to ensure that you are handling your risks and are restricting them to as low as possible. When you adopt a correct strategy and risk management approach, you will be able to make significant profits with day trading, even after making small losses due to a rare bad trade.

15

TIPS FOR INTERMEDIATE FUTURES TRADERS

Being a futures trader, you need to ensure that you clearly comprehend the meaning of a long and a short position. There are several beginner traders who are of the view that profits can only be made when the markets are moving in an upward direction. However, it is important for you to comprehend that futures' trading includes much more than simply keeping up the upward market trend. You should also be aware that being a futures trader, you gain significant benefits when you concentrate on those kinds of assets that have achieved a climax and are at the verge of failure.

When you put your money on an asset during trading, you are said to be selling it short. In other words, it simply refers to the fact that you will call on your broker and buy the rights to access the asset, while hoping to sell it back after a while when its price increases. Keeping in view this definition, we can buy apples in the market for $1 each, and then sell them later for $2 each, which would imply a profit of $1.

When applying this to the real life, $1 can be exponentially multiplied to gain high profits. This is how futures markets function. You are capable of earning significant amounts of money from simple trades.

LONG POSITIONS

Being a futures trader, you are willing to make investments in a certain asset when you adopt a long position in it. The benefits of this position can only be attained when the asset price increases. Being a futures trader, you should have the ability to identify if and when the price of an asset would increase. To be able to do so, you need to understand the essentials of the asset. For example, you need to know about the demand and supply of the market. When you are able to obtain accurate responses to these questions, you can determine if you should make investments or not.

There are essentially specific rules in each market that enable interested parties, like traders, to offer intrinsic value and also to determine the momentum, positive as well as negative. The Central Bank is the major body dealing with currency; hence, those trading in currencies need to be aware of the rules and statements presented by this institution.

The variations in currency in this situation are determined by interest rates. If you believe that there will be an increase in the rate, then it is recommended to adopt a long position on the particular currency. When the interest rates are higher, traders get an incentive to hold an asset for long. This is how the demand for the currency increases, which means that you can sell it at a higher price later and earn high profits.

In terms of stocks and other instruments, the value is driven by the corporations. For example, the worth of a company's stock in the long and short term will be determined by the earnings report. These reports are mostly released each quarter, in which the company executives report their earnings for the previous three months and also their predictions for the future. Hence, if an announcement is made by the company that there will be a decrease in production or plant closure, then a long position should be taken up. This is because a decrease in production will possibly lead to an increase in prices in a few months.

Short Position

In terms of the short position, there are various factors that are the same as the long positions; however, in a reverse direction. Hence, the factors or elements that compel you to select a long position will establish a short position in reverse. For example, when you are willing to invest in currency and there are chances that inflation may decrease, then it would be better for you to adopt a short position for the currency.

In general, when there is indication that inflation is decreasing, it may be determined by the central banks that the interest rates should be decreased to make the financial position of the market consistent. In contrast, when there are higher interest rates, then being a futures trader, you will want to adopt an approach that is adopted by other futures traders. With high interest rates, the prices of products and services are usually higher.

When products are expensive, the sales figure decreases, and this means that the companies will earn less income. Hence, it would be pertinent for futures traders to sell short due to the high rates of interest. Shares and stock indices are few of the instruments that can be sold. This is also how commodities markets and their instruments function. With high rates of interest, there is low demand in the market. This will create the highest chances of commodities like gold and oil selling short in the market.

It is, therefore, recommended to be well aware of the negative factors, as well as those that are considered positive, particularly with respect to your desired asset. This is how you can carry out your research and assessment to decide if you should buy or sell an asset.

Intermediate Futures Trading

Traders having small accounts frequently face problems in making high profits in the futures market. This is not an issue of concern for intermediate traders as leveraging allows them to overcome the issues faced when account size is small.

A successful approach is offered by leverage that allows you to take advantage of your positions. A reliable approach is also offered by leverage that is going to make it possible for you to improve your profit potential when you take full advantage of your trade positions. This implies that you can leverage in a way that you can achieve profits through various means that are not possible in other situations.

Leverage also allows you to achieve maximal gains. However, you should be very careful as leverage is also able to multiply your losses in case any occur. It is quite likely that your market assessment turns out to be incorrect. In such a situation, you may experience losses, which may affect your account. For example, your broker may give you a margin call, which means that you will have to add money to your trading account. If you are not able to add funds to your account, it is going to be suspended.

CONCLUSION

At the end of this guide, I would like to discuss Futures and after-hours trading. Futures and after-hours trading can be examined to determine the way a stock is moving as a key indicator, which may play an important part in determining the entry and exit points in a market. The overall market direction for futures can be shown by S&P and other indexes. You may review after hours trading for individual stocks, particularly when the earnings report is late. This may facilitate you in deciding when to start another trade.

A vital part is played by fundamental assessment in examining buy-and-hold and dividend investors. Swing traders also need to be aware of the profitability of the company in which they are seeking to invest. Technical analysis and reading graphs are the major instruments of trade for the swing trader. You wish to identify trends, alterations in trends and price limitations for stocks as the days pass. This can be carried out using different tools. However, an important tool that is used in the industry is known as "candlesticks". These are basically colored markers on stock modifications, which can be shown for any time period required. For instance, a day trader may observe candlesticks of 1 minute, 5-

minute, 1 hour or 4 hour. Being a swing trader, you may be keen on viewing the daily candlesticks and then following the trends that emerge over the days and weeks. In any situation, candlesticks function in the same way and the same rules are applicable.

Profits will be made by swing traders during the swing of prices, as suggested by the name. One way swing traders can make high profits is by trading powerful trends. However, profits can also be made when a security trades in different prices that is going upwards and downwards among two price levels and not appearing to break out. It is still possible to make profits when the price rises and falls, even though you may be making higher profits when trading trends. This is why majority of the traders prefer to trade trends. There are a few traders who will carry out both kinds of trading, ranges as a normal course of action and trends when they come across such opportunities.

Thank you for taking out time to read this book. Good luck!